A FEELING FOR THE QUICKNESS OF TIME

Poems

by

R. N. TABER

"Colour, creed, sex, sexuality . . . these are but part of a
whole. It is the whole that counts."

First published in Great Britain in 2005 by Assembly Books,
C-Hammond House, 45a Gaisford Street, London NW5 2EB.

Copyright 2005

ISBN 0-9539833-3-1

Typesetting, layout and cover design: ProPrint, Riverside
Cottages, Old Great North Road, Stibbington, Cambs. PE8 6LR

Also by R. N. Taber:

Love And Human Remains: poems - Assembly Books, ©2000
(ISBN 0-9539833-0-7).

First Person Plural: poems - Assembly Books, ©2002
(ISBN 0-9539833-1-5).

The Third Eye: poems - Assembly Books, ©2005
(ISBN 0-9539833-2-3).

DEDICATION

ALICE MAUD TABER
(1916-1976)

Always there for me, believing in me
more than I believed in myself, knowing me
better than I knew myself, loving me
more than I loved myself - though I couldn't
give what you wanted, be what you wanted,
live, love, how you wanted, subscribe
to your fantasy of family unity;
We did our best by each other, assisting
one another through life's maze of emotional
twists, turns, and dead-ends; me, unable
to grasp for years how conflicting loyalties
were tearing you apart. Yours, a divided heart
never truly made whole; we whose demands
you loved to meet always failing it.
Yet, even now, years on since a tumour took
its toll, you are, still, the only one to whom
this son turns, still striving for some peace
of mind, heart, and soul (imagination's
impossible goal) - able to read between lines
to which you alone gave life and meaning.
Only, then, I wasn't listening

Note: Outwardly, my mother was a very ordinary person. Yet
she was a remarkable woman. She gave freely of herself and
received precious little in return.

Much loved by friends and family, no one ever quite understood how she longed to be reassured that she was loved, invariably failing to take such reassurance from the selfish, self-centred way in which those same friends and family often treated her. A naturally loving person, her warmth and understanding extended to everyone she met. She could talk to anyone and everyone enjoyed talking to her – not least about their own lives and problems.

No one has shown me the power of communication more effectively than my mother. She *listened*. Moreover, she could enter into any point of view, even those with which she disagreed. Her gifts were universal although, universally, rarely reciprocated. RNT

CONTENTS

LOVE IS

The L-WORD

DARKNESS AND LIGHT

PINK CLOUDS

WELCOME TO THE 21st CENTURY

THE WORLD TODAY

A FEELING FOR THE QUICKNESS OF TIME

[i] Graham is a very close friend.

[ii] Lorcan is Irish and lives in Dublin. We met in London, 1987.

[iii] I first got to know Michael on the Internet. He and his partner, Frank, live in Devon.

[iv] Bob and Bernie live in California. I first met them on a trip to the U.S. in 1999 when they were celebrating their golden wedding anniversary.

[v] Mike and I were students together in the 1970s.

[vi] Cousin Joan lives in Colorado, USA.

[vii] Dorothy is a dear lady, now in her 90s, who proved to be a good friend at a time of crisis in my life.

[viii] I have got to know Chris on the Internet over several years.

[ix] Aly is also a poet. He lives in Australia and we have exchanged e-mails over several years.

[x] Gary is one of the first people I got to known online before we met up for real in Leeds.

[xi] Linda is a dear friend and colleague who lives in Walthamstow, London.

[xii] Michaela is a friend and colleague.

[xiii] John Paul is the founder of Farrago Poetry. As a direct result of his persuading me to perform an Open Mic at a Farrago event, I have since given poetry readings around the UK.

[xiv] Keith and I became friends in the 6th Form at school in Kent. He later married an Irish girl; they went to live and run a business together in Northern Ireland.

[xv] Barry and I have been friends since 1983. Tragically, his wife Diane died of cancer in 1994. He asked me to include her in this dedication and I am delighted to do so.

[xvi] Andrew is a dear friend and colleague.

PART 1

LOVE IS

LOVE IS

Love is, oh, so beautiful
no matter who, where, how or why,
nor always reciprocal but lets us laugh,
lets us cry, like champagne bringing
a tear to an eye long since made dry
by seasons much like a child's first toys,
treasures once, now barely worth a sigh.
Oh, we get by, our reasons for living
worthy enough and true yet going through
the motions of existence without existing;
getting up, going to bed, getting up again
without kissing sunshine, embracing rain,
warming ourselves at the hot coals
of humanity when struck by the cold
of everyday insanity. We are who we are,
no matter how or why, nor always free
(or able) to sing, laugh, cry, with those
around us - to whom we mean everything.
So let us hear skylarks sing, if not always
the same song, love work a miracle,
no matter whether reciprocal in every
shape or form. Love alone keeps us safe,
keeps us warm. Let the world do its worst,
love will shelter us, nor will its spirit fail
to lead the way, though it shine differently
at the end of this or that tunnel
a light, oh, so beautiful

CRACKING THE CODE

Come a time we die, who'll know
or care (for long) that once we walked
this earth, whose mother gave birth to this
or that child-person as likely as not to
spend a lifetime seeking answers
to questions where there are none, love
taunted by tales of make-believe, peace
where there's but the pain of knowing
how things might have been but for
wasted chances, missed opportunities,
wrong calls as a loaded dice falls on ego's
gaming board, lost chords of pretty songs
meant to make rights out of petty wrongs
(and worse) but merely adding fuel
to flames erasing names from camcorder
tapes of memory wherein we can love,
live forever - so it might be said that, though
dead and gone, here is living proof of lonely
people walking an incredible earth, giving
birth to a world of words, a potential never
quite grasped (principle or purpose)
ghost-talk on the mind, tongue, hopefully
someone taking the trouble to write it down
for others to make sense of, crack the code,
learn from our mistakes, replace a lost chord
or two, discover for what we poets strive,
each human being lives; fickle pursuits
of happiness - or little more than alternatives
to loneliness? Be humanity selfish, selfless,
false or true, flowers of the forest made to cry,
so blessed am I whose soul gave me to you
and you to me though, yes, we die

THE LAST CHAMELEON

Never thought to fall in love again,
as time passes, like kisses in the rain,
sunlight on the sea, moonbeams
chasing shadows, just as we would,
he and I, long gone, a dream to
cherish still though desire perish
like a fire left to smoulder as I
grew older - until I met you and at
first glance, extinguished flames
leapt and began dancing a fantasia
on my heart, feeding its sleeping coals
with such light, such heat, storming
old defences, ravishing me where
I stand for just holding your hand,
engaging your smile, hear old gods
laughing at my heartbeat's frantic
leaping whenever your voice washing
over me, watching lips move that
I long to kiss, wondering what to say
and how to let you know I mean
every word, be sure you understand
the love you inspire in me, conspiring
with a stirring sexuality, no thought of
teasing you, only pleasing you,
new blood coursing through older veins
than yours but no reason for not
winging Avalon's towers, if only in the
sheer poetry of our being together,
whatever you decide, whether returning
these feelings I have for you the same
or choosing to give yours another name;
No matter. Love, friendship, company
of soulmates, our lifelines joined together

or passing at tangents to each other...
Fate, sure to have its wicked way with us,
happy, wishful, sad, ecstatic; a magic
roller coaster running madly, truly, deeply
for, however you choose to respond,
every moment worth the sharing, caring,
laughing, giving and taking that is love
in all shapes and forms, chameleon once
thought lost, returned home at last

INCREDIBLE JOURNEY

Though love blessed, it can hurt,
its wounds fester, let in snake venom;
jealousy, bitterness, hate even...
in a lonely, wretched heaven;
Mostly, though, sadness creeps in,
killing off dark angels one by one,
its twilight as rich as Love's own,
broody silences a bittersweet pain;
Yet, listen! Birds, flowers, Old Man
in the clouds...singing of life, hope,
sunsets, sunrises, spring mists and
summer showers, autumn leaves
of red and gold, fabulous stories
at winter fires told...of love eternal,
no trace of self-pity, only thanks for
making its incredible journey

THE ZEN OF WINDOW CLEANING

Love, more than a word
for the choosing;
window on a world
opening, closing

Look out and count faces
coming, going - departed;
Look in on familiar places,
old friends revisited

Word and world in danger,
bad dreams on cue;
reflections, like anger
distorting our view

Words, learning and unlearning;
world's window cleaning...

VOICE OF A ROSE

Love gave me a rose,
hands signing
in a summer breeze
like petals waving

Its petals dropped
like heaven's tears,
hands at my side
pricked by thorns

See thorns draw blood,
love's fingers staining,
its mind a rising flood
of frantic dreaming

Dreams, like parodies
of summer roses

THE BORROWERS
(For Graham)

You lay a head on my shoulder,
a fragrance in the hair
stirring feelings in me I thought
long gone, never to be
a part of me again. I was wrong.
This heart bursts into song,
yet sadly, for such love cannot be
as I would wish but must
settle for - what? Not less, for that
would suggest second best
and you will always be a treasure
in my heart above all else,
to prize, be glad for each time
I see a light in your eyes
smiling into mine, tears even
for waves of hurt rising
like a flood in you while I can but
do my best with mere words
to assist, inspire, reassure,
lend a shoulder to trust, an arm
to lean upon, embrace you
as friend to friend, longing to hold
and kiss you yet unwilling
to dare risk more (far more) than
I could bear to lose - your love,
although not as I would have it,
in many ways more beautiful
for that. Nor be still, this passion
that stirs in me but ever grow,
lend you to me in ways no body
can hope to know or memory
daub a question mark on history's

blurring sight. No love more dear
than watching the antics of a heart
deserving, oh, so much better
than resting here on my shoulder

NAILS: A CONFIGURATION

Love is kind, blessed with truth
but can lie, be cruel,
yet its passions our dreams fulfil
if we dare choose but allow,
break away - now! - from ties
that bind us to those hopes,
dreams, half truths that are as nails
in our flesh where we hang on a cross of our own design,
tears of blood dripping from a body
waiting for release, unable to pray
but, rather, become as ashes
scattered on self-styled sacred clay;
Or come we down from the cross,
find another way to love...
nor fear its warmth and joy - but
give and take the very spirit
of our mortality, a joining in mind,
body and soul, nor feeling guilty
that pain plays but a bit part in this
epic drama of our lives, happy
to be held close, trusted, comforted,
encouraged to be all we are
and still may be? Though love's kiss
we might not (yet?) return with the
same heat, nor let us count this a loss
but cling, for dear life, to its cross

9

A POPULAR MISCONCEPTION

As far as the eye can see, waves leaping
fantastically, like a pride of unicorns in
a fairy story, rushing to the rescue,
risking all to save the likes of me from
being mere thrall to giants (no such thing
as nine-to-five any more, just working
at keeping wolves from a persistent
sniffing at the door); prisoners of self,
bound to paper promises, unable to see
wood for trees, nor a unicorn for horizons
far and wide, lord of all surveyed, cannot
believe in a heart on the sleeve but taking
it to mean true love, worth working at,
sharing dreams, make them real, world our
oyster. Yet, you sought but a pearl as the
ultimate prize and, sadly, your slave could
not provide so you left my side to seek
elsewhere, up to my eyes in a debt I shall
never square, for you showed me love, in
all its glorious pain. Be sure I will never
let it sin, victorious, again…

SEASON OF SILENCES

One long, lovely summer
once I spent with you
till fallen angels broke cover;
enter autumn, on cue

Our time together near over,
we were as leaves
on a grieving sycamore
falling like tears

Drifting, piling on a grave
of broken promises,
all the love we'll never have
for all our kisses

Saddest of autumn dreams,
unspoken poems

THE ENEMY WITHIN

Love turned its back on me
yet wouldn't run away
but left me nailed to a tree
(couldn't even pray)

Pain alone set me free
to fight another day;
Love, my sworn enemy,
nails in a god of clay

Better stay angry than grieve,
avoid ties sure to rot,
scars worn on a sleeve
to prove – what?

Love, like war and peace
is down to each of us

FLOTSAM AND JETSAM

Love hadn't touched me
for many years;
I'd let myself drift freely
on a sea of tears

Chanced to find peace
(or did it find me?)
and sought to anchor us
in that same blue sea

Sea of sadness, no more;
Blue, only the sky;
Soul once bruised and sore,
bright as a swallow's eye

To shore, at last, homing in
on your heart's outline

BROWN SHOES

Brown leather shoes at the bottom
of my stairs, somebody knocking
at the door but nobody here to answer
so it opens of its own accord,
lets a body enter, back where you
belonged before angels came,
took you away, that awful Thursday
(should have been a mine-and-yours day)
anniversary of our first meeting
in the park; we were walking, got talking,
came to an understanding of sorts
that led to one thing then another
yet it might as well have been a dream
for all that's left of us now, a pair of shoes
at the bottom of my stairs, pleading to be
strolled once more. But there's no returning,
for all this heart's yearning and our front
door's opening of its own accord to let
you back in, where you belong, with me;
Even so, life goes on, like love…
and though I am nobody now you're gone,
to somebody else I well may turn
one of these days, though they will never
want for a spit 'n' polish, brown shoes
left at the bottom of my stairs

A WEDDING SONG

May love be true, its path
with flowers strewn and leaves
of evergreen, roses too,
the poets say, to bring us joy
along our way - and though none
without a hurtful thorn,
let live, let love,
let's overcome
together

No matter

To this man, this woman
To this woman, this man

Forever

Ah, time! Rarely on our side,
though Love a trusting, blushing bride;
We can but try, our dreams fulfil
as best we can, recall that, after all's
said and done, Time waits on
no man, woman, child even,
though love in freefall
beyond things
temporal

True love, eternal

ADRENALIN

Words of love tumble like Niagara
from heavenly heights, a thunderous roar
of metaphor, simile, rhythm and rhyme,
a wondrous sight, vision to behold...
only to be carried along some eternal river
of the soul about which tales are told
but no one ever goes for fear the Unknown
may prove too much, poetry alone no match
for a frantic tide of mixed emotion, devotion
to themes of love, desire, need, drawing
crocodiles to feed, swallow us whole who dare
take a chance on our dreams; instead, we act
the sightseeing tourist snapping for the album,
keeping a diary of Nature's unsubtle cut
and thrust, mocking the foibles of humanity
with such sheer profanity that we hear old gods
laugh, call out names (meant to provoke us
to take action?) as we but watch in awe, give
imagination its due, soaked in the spray
of an elixir of youth, testament to the truth
of our inhibitions if we but care to admit,
rise above, meet the death-defying challenges
of life and (most of all) love's finer glory,
never-ending story of a waterfall...

BLACKBIRD HAS SPOKEN

Blackbird
on a leafy, swaying branch;
Forefinger coaxing
tired nipples, snickering
sparrows rippling our
personal space;
Feisty fingers
at shirts, belts, stubborn zips;
Late spring scents
teasing far suppler thighs
than ours and, yes,
we'll miss that train,
the board meeting
at ten - and leave the curtains
open, closing eyes for
a blackbird's renewed joy
at such a coming alive;
Common body,
three-in-one, grave decisions
celebrating acts
of redemption, blackbird's
finest hour - throat throbbing,
wings flexing;
Now, in full flight,
flung free of tree and branch
to sweeps of sky;
Will settle soon enough
but never for less again
than this

ODE TO SUMMER

Waking in darkness,
walking in pain,
seemed to go through life
seeking love in vain
till one fine morning
while the dew fresh
and clear, smell of roses
in a light, summer air,
we got chatting by and by
at a place near a river
where the willows
never cry

Laughing in the sunshine,
listening to the birds,
first time in a long time,
no loss for words;
Heard grasshoppers singing
while the dew fresh
and clear, smell of roses
in a light, summer air;
We got kissing by and by
at a place near a river
where the willows
never cry

FRIENDS REUNITED

I knocked at the door,
again, again, yet again;
no one came

Eventually, I turned away,
drifted lonely as a cloud
then returned

I banged on the door
again, again, yet again;
no one came

Angrily, I turned away,
ran till exhausted
then returned

I yelled at the door
again, again, yet again;
no one came

Sadly, sat down on a step
left pondering - why
no one listening?

I called at the door
again, again, yet again
till someone came

CATCH ME IF YOU CAN
(For Lorcan)

Poets have strived to catch me;
But how to capture a lark's song
bursting on the ear with mere
simile, metaphor, rhyme...
or convey a rousing waltz in time
to the rhythm of a spring breeze
playing for the coming again
of all things bright and beautiful,
all creatures, great and small?

Painters have strived to catch me;
But how to capture the blue of a sky
on a summer's day, or its hues
of red and gold at the sun's setting
on a glorious reawakening
to the beauty of life, for all its ups
and downs, treasures lost and found,
hopes dashed, sure to be recovered
if only we look long and hard?

Musicians claim to have caught me
in an embrace of song whose beauty
must surely equal the sweet lay
of a nightingale at the closing of a day
seen all that's best in Man and Beast,
the worst forgotten, let fade away
like blood stains in a weeping sky
spelling out the names of those
among us sure to die

Dearer by far than all we own
is love's setting, not its stone

CHORALE

Brooding sky, quiet beach,
love within a fingertip's reach
yet as distant, too, as a watery sun
intent upon closing down the world
everywhere but here, where we are
enjoying a long, beautiful day,
each in our own way, at Nature's
whim, knowing that, for me,
no finer pleasure though I dare say
your thoughts elsewhere (with someone
else? I can but guess). Feisty waves
empathising with my lot, yes, but
performing no sad chorale,
confident I am happy you've chosen
to be with me, whatever the reason,
a glorious day to treasure . . .
Later, twilight's bitter-sweet requiem
spilling hearts already full into nether
regions of the soul, releasing a dove
no more likely to wing true than
this, our fantasia of love. Darkness
closing in. Frantically, we're hugging,
kissing, time against us, fast train
pumping adrenalin, dying man
passing through Avalon

Dvorak in Eastbourne

[Eastbourne, Sussex (UK) March 2004 - see also *Immortal Voices*]

SLEEPING DOGS

Love never dies, nor friendship
but sometimes both lie sleeping
within a heart grown weary,
behind eyes brought to weeping
for all the things that are not as
we would have them and though
accepted, understood, forgiven,
never quite forgot but left asleep
in the arms of every dreamer who
ever loved or had a friend where
love, friendship neither returned
in kind, or even part if we include
unknowing damage to the heart,
ignorance of a crisis of the soul
that love nor friendship can impart
to a mind open only to its own
desires, fires of inspiration, little
more than flames of desperation
a reaching-out for an ideal, dressing
up every opportunity in regalia
appropriate to the same, letting us
see, spectators by any other name,
so we'll appreciate (only too well)
what we're up against, we friends,
would-be lovers even, left waiting
at the gate, knowing it will never
open or, if it should, by courtesy of
some kind fate, the chances are it
will be too late - for rarely will lost

friendships and loves, though stirring
in quiet hearts every now and then,
chance returning to how things were,
might, once upon a time, have been

PUPPETS, STRINGS 'N' THINGS

What to do when so-called friends
keep letting us down, demanding of us
this 'n' that, being around when we long
to run, put miles between us and those
who only give a damn about themselves,
pretend to care ('cause it's the right thing
to do) hoping we won't see through
the charade but play along (as too often
we will) giving benefit of doubt because
we are who we are and others know
(yes, only too well) how to pull strings,
make us do things to their advantage,
whether or not justifiable, so long as we
stay pliable, always on hand, no matter
the rights 'n wrongs of (whatever) 'cause
friends stand by each other, regardless,
and won't ever grass?

Friend, enemy, know ourselves

EUROPEAN UNION
(For Michael & Frank)

Old world, fallen apart;
Panic, a furnace in the heart
fuelled by fears for
a body 's failing strengths
though the spirit fighting
back, always game;
Love, a half-forgotten name
bursting to come again,
aching to soften the blows,
help ease the pain;
Friends, like bluebells, giving
the lie to utter desolation in
spite of a growing desperation
(where now?); salvation
ringing in each ear, the way
unclear. Suddenly, rescue
for two travellers, at least, on
life's super highway,
anxious to rest weary heads,
hungry minds, refresh the heart
with love's no-sweeter wine,
a coming together, finding
each other, shining faces
turning to the sun for more,
far more, than a sense of direction
or body heat (Venus in transit);
Looking forward in love, hope,
peace, come rising stars to
guide and bless the finest union
of all, between people,
on whom, alone, this sad world
turns and a better place

for hearts fired, souls inspired
to seek, find, dare embrace
its rarer gifts, bring happiness,
mend fences, end prejudices

GOOD COMPANIONS

The earth, it smelled of spring and daffodils
as we wandered country lanes, you and I;
Sunshine, clouds and a blackbird's cheery trills,
our good companions to let live, let die

We paused to watch a rich harvest gathered,
let raucous laughter lift heart, mind and soul
till with our good companions we soared
over land and sea, Avalon our goal

Gentle island mist in view, such fragrance!
Descending now on a bed of flowers;
No palace chamber such magnificence
or fine city its heavenly towers

Sun, clouds, blackbird gone. Now just you and I,
dearest companions to let live, let die

FIN

Thinking of you
how we'll never meet again,
turns this sunny world
shadowy, like a shark's fin
heading for me...
intending to kill, end my pain?
Suddenly, the fin darts off
at a tangent to this heavy heart,
unexpectedly lightening
the load, letting me swim ashore
where I hear laughter,
glimpse bare feet dancing
in pools of sunshine...
and though my love for you
courses each pulsing vein,
I know, now, I can live
without ever seeing you again
for ours is the laughter,
ours are the feet in pools
of sunshine we'd dig out of sand
with our own bare hands
time and time and time again,
undeterred by Man, God...

Or, fin?

THE L-WORD

L-WORD
(For Bob & Bernie)

L-ove is a mystery
above all things,
ecstasy or misery

Poor though we be
or walk among kings,
L-ove is a mystery

Who can say, see
to whom life brings
ecstasy or misery?

Around earth's history
running rings,
L-ove is a mystery

Sharing heaven's glory
like a bird that sings,
ecstasy or misery

The one eternity
of life's mixed blessings,
L-ove is a mystery,
ecstasy or misery

ON THE FACE OF WHOM I LOVE

On the face of whom I love, a sweet light
reminding of gay flowers come springtime,
blue hyacinths, red tulips, lilies white,
where rabbits hop, lovers stop and birds sing

On the face of whom I love, a bright light
reminding of sandcastles come summer,
blue skies, ice cream cornets, spade and bucket,
gulls winging, waves lapping at our laughter

On the face of whom I love, a pale light
reminding of snowfalls come autumn's wake,
cosy fires of remembrance burning bright,
bringing joy and peace for a cold world's sake

On the face of whom I love, heaven's kiss…
all things in life that, come dark death, I'll miss

FOR THE LOVE OF LOVE

Though we love to take love into our care,
ask little but to be loved in return,
Love, for its part, does not always play fair,
its kiss inclined to haunt us, tease and burn

Though we love to take love into our care,
keen to nurture, watch it bloom, fulfil us,
Love, by its very nature, cannot bear
the full weight of another's intentions

Though we love to take love into our care,
its own freedom, too, deserves our respect
nor of its weaknesses should we despair
or temples to its shortcomings erect

Though we love to take love into our care,
of its turning jailer, let us beware

HOROSCOPE

Some turn to love but for escape, comfort,
weary of a world full of pain and hate,
sick of being told what to do, (or not),
seek peace, understanding in a kind heart

Some find the escape and comfort they seek,
believe themselves safe under sheltering skies;
some, disenchanted by love for love's sake,
tire of the same people, places, half lies...

Squaring up to life's clout, never easy,
squaring up to love, harder still by far;
looking both in the eye with honesty
demands the sureness of a guiding star

Though to ashes and dust fall our bodies,
in the stars, always, love, life and choices

THE CAPTIVE HEART

Feeding on Nature's skin,
exploring our sexuality;
captive within

Trying, anxiously, within,
for a new reality;
feeding on Nature's skin

Seeking inspiration,
a kinder morality;
captive within

Surpassing expectation,
risen to ecstasy;
feeding on Nature's skin

A sense of valediction
on our mortality;
captive within

A lasting benediction
on love's complicity;
feeding on Nature's skin,
captive within

A POEM IN THE MAKING

When you are lying very close to me
and my fingers are playing with your hair,
I could stay like this through eternity,
so full this poet's heart with love and care

The warmth of your body inspiring me
to write sonnets on the walls of my heart,
my spirit rising to such ecstasy...
it will not contemplate that we should part

Alas, part we must, and this spirit weep
though these eyes stay dry or you may discern
how I dream of us, awake and asleep,
for some lessons some lovers never learn

Yet missing you makes you a part of me
and our lives, though separate, poetry

SUPPER WITH LEO
(For Mike S.)

A great painting,
like supper with a friend,
says everything

Eating, drinking,
living, loving without end;
A great painting

Promising, denying,
sharing wine with a friend,
says everything

Giving, taking,
those trying hours we spend;
A great painting

Believing, disbelieving
what's seen, heard to the end,
says everything

Passion, suffering,
though death, too, a friend;
A great painting
says everything

ON THE ART OF AUTOBIOGRAPHY

There's a reality that's but a dream,
kept within life's quickly turning pages;
though an amateur fiction it may seem,
imparts a wisdom worthy of sages

The lonely man, woman, finds a loved-one
to share life's adventures, emerge heroes;
Failures succeed beyond expectation;
The poor live out their lives in TV shows

Some selves we show the inquisitive world,
others people close to us may perceive;
though of a mind to stay true to falsehood,
no kinder heart, intention to deceive...

Half the world living on expectation,
the rest surviving imagination

BEATING THE PLOTTERS

I must leave you for just a little while;
Relax and enjoy a nice cup of tea;
Go for a walk in the park, laugh and smile,
Play soccer with the lads and think of me

I must leave you for just a little while;
Go find a game of pool, see a movie;
Don't mope about or keep a low profile;
Think positive, have fun, and think of me

I must leave you for just a little while
but I promise we'll be together soon
so don't cry, put on your very best smile,
no matter a cold wind or pouring rain

For all Death's plotting against Happiness
Love is stronger and will resurrect us

THE MIND HEARS, THE HEART LISTENS

Though death have its way
with each of us,
let love have its say

Eyes shut, dare pray
for happiness...
though death have its way

Whatever - come what may
(a fear of emptiness...?)
let love have its say

Duty, too, its passion may
speak up for us,
though death have its way

Dark secrets kept at bay
or homing in on us,
let love have its say

Eternity, a breath away;
Listen for angel voices;
Though death have its way,
let love have its say

BEAUTIFUL THING

Though a day be my last on God's good earth
and I regret many things I have done,
I'll bring hopes of a second chance, rebirth,
to whatever we like to call 'heaven'

Though a breath be my last in Nature's arms
and the world's judgement upon me unkind,
I'll submit to her dear, evergreen charms,
trusting in Peace to be always at hand

Though these eyes look their last on a bird's wing
as it soars with grace and kisses the sky,
I'll clasp to my heart love's beautiful thing
that has blessed me and will not let us die

For knowing you, needing you, loving you,
falls a seed in the wind borne free and true

UNREQUITED

Eyes, feigning sleep;
Soul, turning to you;
Heart, starting to weep

Thoughts I cannot keep
from rushing through...
Eyes, feigning sleep

Words of love I'd heap
tenderly on you;
Heart, starting to weep

Arms that would hold, keep
you safe eternity through;
Eyes, feigning sleep

Desire, creature of the Deep
no man can subdue;
Heart, starting to weep

In dreams, such joy to reap
a harvest rare and true;
Eyes, feigning sleep;
Heart, starting to weep

WAITING FOR SOMEONE

I waited for you, who did not arrive
and the supper I had prepared went cold;
Days, weeks, months, years later - and still I grieve
for the pain I endured, the lies you told

I waited for you, who did not arrive;
like autumn leaves our love turned, faded, fell,
drifted a while, unable to survive
jealousy's blast, blowing mad and cruel

I waited for you, who did not arrive
and now we're both lonely, grown old, mellow,
our togetherness but dreams in a sieve
shaken by a sandman on love's pillow

I waited for you who did not arrive,
nor few happy times since have long to live

THE HUNGRY HEART

Someone, anyone, needing me,
a fine way to get by...
loneliness feeding on me

Voices, cruelly, mockingly
demanding - why...
someone, anyone, needing me?

Choices, always goading me
to expose a white lie;
loneliness feeding on me

Scathing home truths at me
to get real, deny...
someone, anyone, needing me

No one about to set me free,
though a sandman try;
loneliness, feeding on me

Love, a life and death poetry
milking rhyme, reason, dry;
Someone, anyone, needing me;
loneliness feeding on me

SWEET DREAMS

I sat with you and watched the stars appear,
saw the moon sail like a yellow balloon
where singles weep and only lovers dare,
riding white horses on sunset's ocean

We reached an island of candyfloss clouds,
breached its peppermint reef to a fair shore
far, far away from the world's cares and crowds
warning that love is but a myth, a whore

No cruel words here of faithlessness and pain,
only sweet kisses that last forever,
my joy evergreen, your tears like spring rain,
a bonding temporal hurt can't sever

Our dreams, down to earth, come dawn's frosty glow;
Our love, no myth, a flower sure to grow...

INVISIBLE MAN

Alone in the rain,
heaven knows why;
Invisible man

A sickening pain
as commuters rush by,
alone in the rain

A mere stain
on earth and sky;
Invisible man

Craving someone
to notice I cry
alone in the rain

Praying no one
will see how I die;
Invisible man

Shot down the sun,
kissed you goodbye;
Alone in the rain,
invisible man

THE TRUTH ABOUT LOVE

My true love gave to me a yellow rose
that I would always recall in my heart
how love, if tended, nurtured, always grows
like the truth only wisdom can impart

My true love gave to me an apple green
so I would recall with each eager bite
that what was, is now, and always has been
since the Tree of Knowledge stole Eden's light

My true love gave to me a gentle kiss
to which my soul responded with its all;
leaves, petals, embracing childhood summers,
reaching for the sky, God's heaven its goal

My true love passed away some years ago
but lives on in me, truly, this I know

A FAILING LIGHT

Walking in the park,
chatting with you
as it gets dark

I hear dogs bark,
a sad dove coo,
walking in the park

Winter, chill and stark,
like my life with you
as it gets dark

Once we heard a lark,
swore a love that's true
walking in the park

No need for small talk,
enough to be with you
as its gets dark

Now, barely a spark
in heaven worth the view,
walking in the park
as it gets dark

MOVING ON

Only for you the most beautiful song
this sad heart of mine can hope to compose,
a hymn to true love ever rich and strong,
like the sweet smells of summer in a rose

Only for you the most beautiful words
this lonely soul of mine can hope to write,
echoes in the wind, love song of the birds,
a stirring of petals come dawn's first light

Only for you this broken heart's mending,
remembering a promise to move on;
though love come again, ours never ending
like the lifelines on twin leaves evergreen

Keeping faith with you till the end of time;
my life, a love song, your death, my poem

THE ZEN GUIDE TO EATING OUT

Bright and breezy,
a good place to eat,
light and airy

A hint of strawberry,
old friends to meet,
bright and breezy

A touch of history
on the Sandman's beat,
light and airy

Green leaves of memory,
fragrant and sweet,
bright and breezy

On wings of eternity
sad world sure to quit,
light and airy

A passing reality
to keep the mind quiet;
Bright and breezy,
light and airy

LOVE ON THE TURN

I love him and though he does not love me,
no matter, because love is not as blind
as some would have it - and my heart can see
past its dreams, the scalding touch of his hand

Our kisses lack passion - we are but friends;
each hug, a fantasy for which he yearns;
poor substitute for impossible ends,
altar candles where his lonely heart burns

I long for our hugs, the sound of his voice,
his guitar, our lovemaking, my secret...
since he's already made a lifetime choice,
for all else (and whom) no real time or thought

It's love's dark side, conspiring to meet needs
greater than the friendships on which it feeds

PASSION, PRIDE AND POETRY

The first, most passionate love in my life
taught me to believe in myself, walk tall;
though others warning of such pain and strife
I knew it was this, or nothing at all

The first, most passionate love I embraced
taught me to be true to my heart's desire;
though others warning of a soul disgraced,
I kept faith, warming my hands by its fire

My first, most passionate love in a world
that scorns me, even now, for being gay,
saves me from cut and thrust of cruel word,
no matter the worst some people may say

That first, most passionate love I feel still,
taking shape in a poem, always will

OCEAN CROSSINGS
(For Cousin Joan)

See the ocean on a fair summer's day,
gentle waves kissed by the sun's golden light,
a kindness of dolphins come into play,
ballet of an albatross in full flight

See the ocean when the sky in a rage,
mighty crescendo of waves bearing down
like terrified beasts, driven to rampage
by Man's compulsion to steal Nature's crown

See the ocean when stars shining brightly,
the moon sailing boldly where angels fear,
dark swell spawning the same brute history
that brought us, laughing, weeping, praying here

Oceans apart, let's follow freedom's cry...
swimming with dolphins and learning to fly

PART 2

DARKNESS AND LIGHT

A PENNY FOR THE RAT-CATCHER

Within these walls, grown impatient
for retribution although we know
only too well it's no solution
to lively contractions of the soul,
petty constrictions on the heart,
predictions in the stars once easily
dismissed but now conveniently
allied to human premise
however perverse

Keeping the enemy at bay, without
or within - that's the question?
Haunting dreams that dare defy
the rationale of hurt pride,
disaffected ego, demanding
satisfaction but unwilling to display
its true colours, fearing others
might fly their own, the worse
to win us over

No better self-perpetuating poison
could Mother Nature produce
nor God induce even the likes
of Eve to inflict on humanity
than this cancerous vainglory,
rodent feelings scuttling
through tunnels of a mind
but poorly lit, heading
for self-destruct

Like the rat-catcher in our sewers,
hate perseveres

ONLY NATURAL

Brighter than home fires
in a storm;
Finer than down on
a swan;
Sweeter than honey
on the tongue;
More durable than trees
left alone, spared
planning permission

Stronger than the fiercest
elements;
Tougher than any fibre,
man-made or gossamer
of Nature;
Like a hurricane, it rears
over earth and sky;
All appears tranquil, safe
in its eye

Lovelier than springtime;
Longer than summer;
Gentler than autumn;
Sleepy as winter - yet
beware the bear that wakes
too soon at some foreign
intrusion on its patch,
more than a match
for anyone

No greater wisdom or folly
than loyalty

DARKNESS AND LIGHT

Though death's dark canopy
our lives obscure,
to light, the victory

Along thorny paths of history
we'll tread with care
though death's dark canopy

Whose choices easy
or conscience clear?
To light, the victory

Of life's prevailing mystery,
to love the greater share
though death's dark canopy

For all that pain and misery
may humanity obscure,
to light, the victory

Eternity, no enemy…
(of this, be sure);
Though death's dark canopy,
to light, the victory

DAWN CHORUS
(For Dorothy H.)

Today will be a good day
happen what might;
love and truth, the way

Nor shall grief hold sway
over the longest night;
today will be a good day

Let loneliness find its way
into heaven's light;
love and truth, the way

Though a sandman say
we stay out of sight,
today will be a good day

As written in God's clay,
know wrong from right;
love and truth, the way

Pain, guilt, our Calvary
as earth's ills we fight;
Today will be a good day,
love and truth, the way

TALKING WITH LAZARUS

Death reached out a hand, soon stroking my hair,
refused to go away, insisted on staying near
to where I lay on a bed of grass, fallen like a leaf,
its season past, shelter taken, much pleasure too
where hopefully sought, for no small treasure, this
among Nature's gifts, freely given to bring us
closer to heaven as we look up, see the splendour
of a tree, browse the beauty of a poetry evergreen
though the tree be deciduous, autumn no less
insidious a predator as time itself, feeding upon
the temporary nature of things, surrendering
(on the face of it) to an Ending, refusing to go away,
insisting on staying near, making sure we cannot
help but feel its hand stroking the hair, hear Sirens
in the ear offering more, far more than we find
here on a bed of grass, our season past – though
let us not forget how even one dead leaf returns
to the earth, food for rebirth, harbinger of spring
in spite of everything threatening to destroy us,
steal our shelter, pleasure too, undermine the hope
we seek when all around, like winter, seems but
as cold and bleak as tales told about death, beguiling
hearts, minds, souls grown weak from struggling
to cling to a single branch, battered by winds, season
after season, finally (apparently) bested for no other
reason than its being nature's way so what choice
kinder than to take the hand that strokes the hair,
plucks the leaf from its tree, ensures things are as
they're meant to be? Ah, but we are not as fallen
leaves on a bed of grass but blessed with more than
sunshine, rain and nesting songs to see us through
the rights and wrongs of temporal seasons, nor should
we fear Death's hand or voice since, unlike a leaf,

we are blessed with choices (if choices we care to
make than trust to Fate) and though we fall, listen out
for memories rustling like leaves stroking the hair,
reading poems in the ear

So let's arise this soaking bed of grass and go forth,
talking with Lazarus

NAILS: A HISTORY

For life, love, beauty, peace and more than this
a man called Jesus came into the world,
betrayed, not by the sword but by a kiss
yet, centuries on, some still keep His word

Written in clouds, mist, sunlight, falling leaves,
where snowflakes are drifting, home fires burning,
for he and she who laughs, sings songs or grieves,
there's life, love, beauty, peace everlasting

At a Father's house of many mansions
Mother Nature pays due thanks and prayer
on our behalf, no matter religions,
for life, love, beauty, peace enough to share

Pity life, love, beauty, peace and much more,
hammered home on nails at History's door

BLUEGRASS BUDDHA

Cross-legged on the sands of time,
wishing the tide away,
watching the flotsam, jetsam
of long, happy hours
swoop and dive like gulls
chasing crumbs thrown
by this child, those watchers,
from a sandcastle's tower
on a blue glass sea of dreams;
Oh, happiness, reminding
like specks in a kaleidoscope
even as it turns, like earth
around the sun, of days gone
forever, never to return!
Good, bad, halcyon days
chasing after crumbs
thrown by this child-watcher
from a castle of half lies
on a bluegrass sea of dreams
listening to The Man play,
wishing the tide away

CAVE PEOPLE, 3000 AD

Though temporal light fall into darkness,
melting icecaps flood village, town, city,
may the same love of life creating us
keep its flame burning through eternity

Though prayer seem to fail us, God abscond
as we fall victim to worldly desires,
let there be candles all over this land
guiding us to kinder, far safer shores

Though we turn our backs on forest and beast
without any thought for their tomorrows,
may our grandchildren, at the very least,
keep a flame burning in Heaven's towers

Though bats winging their way through centuries,
who'll re-invent our own native blindness?

RIGHTS OF WAY

At the gates of heaven
an angel gave me a choice;
enter in a state of grace
or return, for better or worse,
make good mistakes
yet to be made, watch plans
fall apart still to be laid,
risk all - for love, wealth,
position, whatever it takes
for one of any disposition
to justify a decision

At the gates of hell
an angel gave me a choice;
toss a coin - heads
or tails? For good or ill,
may heads turn in this
direction, eyes blink opinion
where mouths much prefer
to follow a general direction
rather than cause a stir,
risk all - especially derision
in an open situation

At the gates of love
an angel gave me a choice;
seize the day, come what
may - or play the fool, chance
seeking out the stars alone
baying silently for the moon,
nor shall there be warmth,
or hope at each new day for
turning away from me - kiss

of life, heart beating free

Come hellfire or heavenly light,
be sure to open the gate

WHO MOVED THE STONE?

Who moved the stone,
let in the light;
Heaven, wide open

Grave promises given,
future bright;
Who moved the stone?

Less heavy, the burden;
Restored, our sight;
Heaven, wide open

Fears forsaken,
come cavernous night;
Who moved the stone?

Sins, forgiven;
Love, arisen from hate;
Heaven, wide open

Bringing to religion
an all-embracing light;
Who moved the stone?
Heaven, wide open

SUN WORSHIPPERS

Lying on the sand
letting the sea lick our feet,
listening to waves
like the heartbeat of a god
crashing against
the temple of its Being,
sending adrenalin
flowing through the veins
of acolytes thinking
to serve a Higher Power
than priests playing
games of their own - with
other people's lives,
thoughts, ideas, let alone
the faith that inspires
man, woman, child, across
land, sea, air, to bring
their joys, sorrows, hopes
for a better life...
to the altar of self-sacrifice,
spread arms, legs,
heads bowed, eyes closed
listening for that
still small voice, priestly
ritual superimposed
to encourage a sense of being
at one with Creation,
one nation beneath a heaven
that can only watch
helplessly as we lie on sand,
letting waves tickle toes
and (who knows?) learning
to understand...

KNOW THE VOICE, CAN'T PLACE THE FACE

Come, child, where I lead,
don't be afraid;
Listen to the murmurings
of your heart;
Exercise the finer leanings
of your mind;
Start to care, understand
why I, too, am here
for you

See, child, where I walk;
Let's talk, you and I,
exchange home truths
that, otherwise, may well
fester and die in the bowels
of a soul bent on proving
its existence by a token
resistance to temporal
magnificence

Hear, child, such words
as your own; ignore mine
if you suspect they threaten
the ivory tower you build
with such pretension, desire
to be alone hardly the best
protection against a world
its own worst enemy for
a divided humanity

Part godly, part devilry,
call me Destiny

CASCADE

In the dark of night I stumbled along
the lonely, winding passages of birth,
no star nor moon or night bird's fragile song
as, naked, I was summoned to the earth

Come history's first light, I'd dried my tears
to make those who fed, clothed, cradled me - proud;
By noon I had joined a stream of refugees
pleading sanctuary of Man's frail God

In the twilight of my years, I found peace
though not in a world obsessed with terror
but in cascades of springtime feeding trees,
guiding birds, bees, from flower to flower

Come death, no need for night bird, moon or star;
in love's cascade, we'll sing, shine, forever

LEGENDS OF THE FALL

Creed, tradition, ritual,
more, far more than
celebrations spiritual

Either side of a wall
on the site of our pain;
creed, tradition, ritual

Does God's battle call
bring us to decision,
celebrations spiritual?

To keepers of the wall
let knowing fingers turn;
creed, tradition, ritual

Mosque, cathedral,
synagogue; common stone,
celebrations spiritual

Legends on every wall
to our own design;
Creed, tradition, ritual,
celebrations spiritual

PRO-LIFE

I hear voices
in the darkness,
crying out to me, protesting
how mortality would
strike us down before we're ready;
now can only watch in secret
as others attempt to take on
what once we - hopefully - began,
spirit willing though flesh
but an anonymous wannabe,
subject to debate though
no opportunity to speak up
for itself about all it risks
missing out on - like
learning to speak, count,
get along with people, whatever
colour, creed, sex, sexuality;
experiencing achievement
worthy (maybe) of acclaim
or at least applause;
discovering love, its many joys
and pitfalls, better to know
than made to forgo, never get
to feel the ecstasy of being
soul to soul, heart to heart,
body to body with someone
caring more for me than you
it seems, though I haunt
your dreams, night and day,
for believing I hadn't the right
to stay though who's to say
whose word gives whom
the keys to this world

or what manner of world it is
insists we choose?

GOD'S ARCH

Arch of budding leaves
inviting us to explore
where a spring rain gives
hope, even to the poor

Carpet of velvety green
letting us feel richer
than we have ever been
for a sense of summer

Arch of bare branches
like a debt collector
hunched over the profits
of a fickle nature

A FEELING FOR CHRISTMAS

Once
I found a Christmas tree
discarded in the street,
some of its branches cut away,
the rest looking shabby (to
say the least) needles already
turning shades of brown
like crumbs of toast, a sorry
specimen indeed that few
passers-by would have spared
a glance, but something
in me responded to that tree,
so I bent down, picked
it up, took it home, placed it
in a tub of earth and recall
thinking how good it was to
restore a sense of dignity
to the spirit of a sad little tree
which, surely, would die
but not without playing a part
of sorts in Christmas, even
with someone like me, hardly
the smiling face of festivity!
I found two dusty baubles, some
tinsel and a lopsided star.
It seemed to me the little tree
took on an air of triumph,
celebration, things I'd preferred
to forget at this time of year.
By the 25th it had taken root,
a sight for sore eyes indeed,
one I felt a need to share, with
such joy and pride I hadn't

experienced before, not like this
sense of – Christmas?

FACTS AND CANDLE WAX

Even love is suspect,
should it fail to deliver
the trust and respect
we owe one another;
Even love will lie
to save its own dear skin
though a candle die
on the high altar of pain;
Find love, surviving
even a flame snuffed out,
no braver spirit living,
refugee put to rout

PROMISES, PROMISES

Among angry hills,
I promised my heart to worms
then a storm burst and we stumbled
on slopes of grassy mud
to which I promised every last
drop of my blood
then the sun came out again
opening my eyes to birds' wings and miracles
and we got dead drunk on a misty rain, headed home, bare feet
stalling on this ragged stone,
that carpet of thorns...
each one screaming for - what?
Something, someone, a purpose, reason,
sense of resurrection once mist and rain
finally done restoring the sun to its crowning glory
though bits of sky haunted still by clouds emulating
rocks, thorns, unicorns in scattered shapes
and various personae yelling in the ears
to keep running, running, running
or miss the last train, promising that
getting to the station on time
deserves promising in return
to see these feet safely home,
tucked in bed by nightfall,
eyes closing, lips praying
without a sound, angry hills
reminding us we are promised
to earthworms, feeding on
our flesh come night, day, mist, shine.
Nor matters this...
in stormy darkness or the light
of our resurrection

IMMORTAL VOICES

Splendid church, full;
orchestra and choir in place;
Hear a holy silence fall
like an act of grace

Conductor takes the baton,
music starting to grow
like flowers in spring rain
on Ground Zero

To sad hearts, an uplifting
as Dvorak intended;
loved ones returning,
Peace descended

Performance over, task done;
Forever, *Amen*

[Note: Written after attending a Dvorak *Requiem* concert in aid of
the families of British victims of 9/11. Eastbourne, Sussex (UK)
March 27th 2004 - see also *Chorale*]

WARM HANDS, COLD HEART

Icy shrapnel,
a tearful mistiness;
winter's terrible
revenge on us

Frozen bodies
for whom we'll pray;
vainglorious mummies
on display

Death's kiss, surreal;
all sense of ego's rod
abandoned (in a deal
with God?)

Coaxing cosy home fires,
pretending otherwise...

CARE IN THE COMMUNITY

Knocked at an old house
in the Square

Is anybody there?

At a grubby letterbox,
bent to peer

Is anybody there?

Caught a whiff, of
mouldy air

Is anybody there?

A squeaking, (maybe sobs
or mice on the stair)

Is anybody there?

No one replying, prying
curtains everywhere

Is anybody there?

Moving on, plenty more
with time to spare

Is anybody there?

Asking questions no one
wants to hear

HEARTBEAT

Heart's beating (in vain,
an anaesthetizing darkness
at a new dawn)

How to know when
if ever, find happiness?
Heart's beating in vain

Shall sleep's half-open
portals but let in distress
at a new dawn?

Dreamer in pain,
nailed to a centre-cross;
heart's, beating in vain

Fat chance then,
a soul's savouring redress
at a new dawn!

So what light bursting in
divinely, denying this
heart's beating in vain
at a new dawn?

IN LOVING MEMORY

Years on from terror in the sky
and still the same question – why?
What manner of Man is it learns but
contempt for human life, taking
mother from child, husband from wife?
From loving parents - a son, daughter
never thought to outlive...never mind
survive a slaughter

They were places like any other places
at the start of a working day,
faces like any other faces looking
as if to say...roll on home time!
His, telling family responsibilities;
Hers too, but softer, cool...
that the kids will have a good day
at school

Twin towers, gone. Faces linger on,
give us strength that we may live
to hold our heads high and make them
proud of us In Loving Memory;
Reality, crueller than any fairy story
told to generations to distinguish
good from evil. Altar candles, no natural
causes can extinguish

Though unthinkable terror seem to win,
to Love, always, the spoils of its sin

MEMORIES, PRAYERS, FLOWERS

Although my tears falling like winter rain
for thinking of your hurt and suffering,
I think of springtime, see you once again
as we were then - hopeful, happy, laughing

Although my heart cries out in pain, despair,
for the sheer tragedy your plight inflicts,
I think of summertime and see you there,
jumping for joy - despite this life's conflicts

Although I know my prayers will be heard,
I can't be sure of the answers He'll give
but I think of the goodness in His word,
and know He'll always keep us safe, alive

For life is more, much more than this we know;
Love, a flower, in our hearts sure to grow

REQUIEM FOR A POET

When time ceases to be
and all that's left is eternity,
what then will they think of me
who drank my wine at table,
doubted I was able to write
at all or, at least, as well
as one might, who always kept
Mount Parnassus in sight,
despite the English climate?
Oh, I dare say they were right
but I've so enjoyed being a poet,
lapping up every lisping word
of criticism, praise, scepticism,
quips about simplicity,
a lack of intellectuality, how
gay-interest poetry undermines
a proud genre's integrity,
compromises the very aesthetic
of its history, spirituality;
a cardinal sin to lower the tone,
let anyone in on a serious poem,
its place in the Arts clearly meant
to impress, access only partly
allowed - or its mystery solved;
that way anarchy lies. Besides,
a poet must always have the edge
on Mr, Mrs and Ms Average

To death, life's task, my body;
To whom, I ask, my poetry?

DESERT SONG
(For Chris)

Among smoky hills
and burning plain
seek daffodils
in vain

Yet when it's spring
back home...
hear cuckoos sing,
see Nature bloom

So far away it seems
the heart may stray
yet, wrapped in dreams
forever stay

As the finer spirit wills,
a time of daffodils

THE RETURN

Swaying, drunk with life
at the very edge of darkness,
praying to heaven's distant swell
that I may not lose my balance,
fall into this pit of despair, this
hell among ghosts; sure to tumble,
losing the will to live, fight for all
this heart and soul have achieved
in spite of those philistines always
conspiring against voices of prose
and poetry to delete us from living
memory who, along with painters,
music makers, would inspire those
less blessed - to find a place of rest
within themselves, engage with
the artist in a finer art than art alone
can aspire without tongues of fire
sounding out our intention, only
wonder at its invention, take heart
at its ascension into a Heaven of its
own making, ours for the taking if
we dare give rein to free volition,
look to see, read to learn, hear to
listen. Oh, edge of darkness…recalls
such sounds, sights, words, calls me
me back to you, the world, flawed
as we are, the time not yet to grieve
though one day called upon again
like this, to leave. For now though,
I will answer "No" and with Apollo's
first kiss on my lips, to uncertain
bliss, in peace, gladly go…

CANDLES IN THE DARK

When death, she comes for me,
pray, few regrets or tears;
let it be poetry

O, but I shall miss sky and sea,
a south wind's sweeter whispers...
when Death, she comes for me

May love stand by steadfastly
our finest memories;
let it be poetry

O, but I shall miss bird and tree,
such joy Mother Nature inspires...
when Death, she comes for me

May our dreams slip gently
into a bed of flowers;
let it be poetry

Our way, in peace, lit eternally
by candles in heaven's towers;
When Death, she comes for me,
let it be poetry

PART 3

PINK CLOUDS

RITES AMONG MEN

There was a time I was in love with love;
every man I met was the one for me;
Each night I'd gaze at the bright stars above,
wishing for someone to be there for me

Again and again, I mistook lust for love,
reeling from my foolishness, loss and pain
till one night, gazing at those stars above,
you came along, paused, put a hand in mine.

Two lonely men cruising, out for a thrill,
we savoured, believed in that first sad kiss;
your mouth, arms, body heat in for the kill
found me baring my heart for sacrifice...

Old gods applauding among stars above,
we rediscovered ancient rites, made love

PINK CLOUDS
(For Aly M.)

Two men sharing a lovers' kiss
(or two women);
pink clouds are made of this

Your love brought me such bliss
as I'd never known;
two men sharing a lovers' kiss

Now long gone, I still miss
your sweat, your semen;
pink clouds are made of this

We begged the world for peace,
to be left alone;
two men sharing a lovers' kiss

But the world had other ideas,
like persecution;
pink clouds are made of this

Let them try, no one can deny us
a bird's eye view of heaven;
Two men sharing a lovers' kiss;
pink clouds are made of this

BODY BEAUTIFUL

Beads of sweat
on a fine chest, pearly nipples
demanding to be explored,
diving instincts exposing them
to a mind intent on...
an explosion of sexual activity
between legs like jelly,
all-quivering desire making ripples
through this body, so near
yet so far from such perfection
that no erection could last
for long, but needs burst like some
joyous song, hymn to love,
lust, desire - call it what you will
but nothing quite like it,
pounding like gospel on the ears,
filling our eyes with tears
for such beauty in a world much
maligned for an absence
of sensitivity towards whatever
icons we may choose
to invest a body of feeling within,
yearning for free expression
and more, much more, but even now
dripping into oblivion - unless
we open our mouths to say exactly
what we mean, try pricking
the heart of any adversary who
will, for sure, never best
the sheer thrill of licking sweat
on your fine chest...

FRONTIERSMEN

I love to lie naked with you,
letting the warmth of your flesh
invade mine and comfort me,
make me so glad to be - alive!
In an embrace or lying still,
asleep or awake, your nearness
touches my heart as surely
as your lips part to receive my
yearning tongue when we
make love, learning more about
each other and ourselves
during each glorious, intimate
moment as we, in the gutter,
reach for the stars and discover
new galaxies to explore,
plant our seed, express a need
denied all known art forms
for more, far, far more, than sex
and its ready Box of Delights
can expect to offer as we lie here
together, secure in the knowledge
that we are soulmates, bound by
a love beyond mere parameters
of time and space and I gaze upon
your face, content to caress its
outline, lightly, with a forefinger,
knowing that, soon, your smile
will cross new frontiers, lips raise
a cheeky grin before we begin
again, again, to show the world
how it matters far less than our
being here together, like this

ON THE DIVERSITY OF BODY LANGUAGE

The world, it quickly turned its back on me
when I was but a shy, unknowing child,
casting me aside deliberately
were I less than a broken toy, despised

Yet even spare parts may join to inspire
youth's dream of turning water into wine;
mine, too, sights set on ideals, no matter
life's conventionally perverse front line

I found peace at Love's university
scaling much the same learning curve as you,
discovering joy in a poetry
needing no words yet reading sound and true

Whose then the right to reject such as we,
deny gay love spirituality?

TO LOVE, THE VICTORY

I tried to kill my love, it would not die,
banish my emotions, they would not go;
Some said you were the guilty one (not I)
but how are they who've never loved to know?

It takes two to begin a love affair
and two, again, to bring the shutters down;
Yet it takes only one, love's hymn to share
with a heart growing dark and all but done

I begged, please, one more chance to defy them
who always said our love could never be;
Dare I say it's the singers, not the hymn
shall raise us to rousing tunes of glory?

Still, some gossip and spread tales about us
but we (though gay) in love, victorious

COMING TOGETHER

Come light of day
to midnight's soul,
a love that's gay

Dark swept away,
hearts made whole
come light of day

Let us pray,
and glad bells toll
a love that's gay

Cold feet of clay,
a wake-up call
come light of day

Breaking away
from backs to the wall,
a love that's gay

Let the world say
what it will;
Come light of day,
a love that's gay

COME, FLY WITH ME

Some say our love is wrong,
can only end in tears,
as on wings of glorious song
we rise above their fears

Home, school, church, work,
may tolerate us - or worse;
Love's light shines in our dark
to spite convention's curse

No matter what the world says,
anxious to keep face,
those who know and care for us
will keep it in its place

Sticks and stones may hurt us
but truth is where the heart is

WHEN LOVE IS NOT ENOUGH

It was hard on my heart to let you go;
I even stood and watched you walk away;
of the tears I wept you will never know
for your not having the courage to stay

I cannot blame you for the choice you made,
your way of seeing so different from mine;
all you saw was pain and angst to be had,
every step we'd take, every corner turn

You begged me to keep our love a secret
but that was something I just couldn't do;
I saw no shame in us, cause for regret,
longed to tell this sick, sad world I loved you

Many years on, it's still hard on my heart,
your belief, 'cause we're gay, we had to part

DON'T STOP THE CARNIVAL

In Notting Hill
we lost our way
at Carnival

World so colourful
turned a tearful grey
in Notting Hill

By nightfall
we'd had our say
at Carnival

First and last call;
put our masks away
in Notting Hill?

Your face fell
nor would you stay
at Carnival

We said farewell
and you walked away,
in Notting Hill
at Carnival

PERFECT STRANGERS

Shirtfront hung wide open,
red hairs on his chest;
tongues of fire, leaping out
at me, licking at my nipples,
rekindling desire, teasing this
cold heart with dreams once
cherished, long forsaken;
liquid eyes spilling over, soaking
my tee like spring rain, letting
a body breathe again after years
of choking on ashes, living on
flashes of memory...
I long to take this stranger in
my arms, be close to someone
again, yet dare not even ask
his name, can but look, my life
an open book if he but cares
to flick a page or two, sewn
with paper thin threads
of flesh and bone, sure to snap
should he come any closer without
word or sign that I'll not be
tugging at some barely open
door to a heaven that's rarely
let me in before!

Lips parting, tongues peeping,
hearts leaping

A FEELING FOR FANTASY

Strolling by fields of barley, wheat and rye,
my love and I sought lasting rest and peace;
twin spirits hungry for sanctuary,
weary of a world always judging us

We reached woodlands alive with leafy song,
a sonata for lovers everywhere,
paused to ask a tree nymph for its blessing,
keen to turn our backs on urban despair

The nymph warned it was born of the country,
bound by the countryside's own moral code,
had only heard tales of urbanity,
a Grim Reaper harvesting swathes of road

Such peace here! "For us, too, a gay couple?"
"Ah," said the nymph, "*that* depends on people."

SPRING MIST

One spring we strolled by a murmuring stream,
listening to the happy tales it told
of peace and love walking out of a dream
to take their rightful place in a sad world

As we walked, your fingers entwined with mine,
they too with a joyful story to tell
of lonely gay people thrown a lifeline,
saved from drowning in contempt's ugly swell

We paused, saw two fish in a gentle flow,
wished them safe from the angler's cruel rod,
their colours and grace making a fine show
yet vulnerable, like us, in this world

Crossing a bridge, we paused again and kissed,
peace and love embracing us like spring mist

LOVE AND DEATH IN JERUSALEM

The first time I made love to a woman,
it proved - what? Only that I was anxious
to run and tell the world I wasn't gay;
The world was only too happy to listen,
take me back with a joyful cry - but
I suspected it knew I was living a lie;
She was warm, gentle, loving and giving,
a fine catch for any man and, oh, how
I longed to give back all I was taking!
Each time, though, I looked into eyes
bright and shining, lips so inviting...
they were yours, the lovemaking ours;
I didn't want to be gay, had told you so
and you went away. I saw nothing wrong
in convention, although I begged you stay;
Why not have a home, wife, kids,
a secret male lover too? But, no, it was
all or nothing with you so I had to choose,
nor did it seem too hard a decision at
the time. Everyone agreed, a fine couple
we made, she and I - but even lying next
to her in bed, you were on my mind,
haunting my heart, reproaching me so
for letting us part, afraid you had already
found someone else to take my place (yes,
even in the heat of her embrace). In time
of course, she guessed, made me tell all,
bare my soul. Her tears killing us, I could
but humbly ask her forgiveness

"One day - maybe," she said, but then
"Firstly, we must learn to live again."

GREEN FINGERS

Each time I'd look up and see you
smiling from some herbaceous border,
sparrows on the washing line,
daisies on the lawn, sunshine spread
like a burst balloon;
I longed to know for sure what's
in your head? Should I take it as read
that I'm only here to cut the grass,
prune the rose trees, weed the beds,
rid the greenfly...
get the garden looking as it should?
And I would - if only you'd see to that
herbaceous border instead of grinning
at me as if to say other things
need sorting (if I dare?);
So what are we waiting for?
Let's get going right away, the daisies
will still be here another day - and
God already told the sparrows
we're gay...
A lonely Eden, sharing a pain
left unspoken, letting the sparrows'
cheery chorus disguise uneven
ties (unbroken even by
our silences);
Oh, labours of love!
Busy hands in the earth, green fingers
learning about life, death, rebirth,
how you and I can surely
find a way...

Now, looking God and sparrows
in the eye every day

RECONCILIATION

In the water, an ugly face looking up at me,
bags under the eyes, tramlines on the brow,
mouth crooked (in the queerest expression)
firing questions at me that passed over
my head, joined with seabirds making merry
in a summer breeze without touching me
or so much as lightly brushing a moist eyelid
although echoing distantly in my head

In the water, a told-you-so sun looking up at me,
bags under its eyes, reeling from a freak storm
that leapt with little warning as a panther might
stalk and jump its prey. Shivering now in spite
of the afternoon's clammy heat. Oh, I was scared
but stayed put, let the beast sniff and circle me,
stared into the very whites of its eyes, dared it to
do its worst - but it moved on, left me alone

In the water, your dear face looking up at me,
bags under the eyes, tramlines on the brow,
mouth crooked (in the queerest expression)
putting answers to me that whirl inside
my head, join with seabirds making merry
in a summer breeze, breathing life into me,
drying a moist eyelid, passion on my tongue
like the lyric of our favourite love song

Reconciled, we'll stroll the lake's leafy shore,
scared of being gay and in love no more

TEARS FOR FEARS

I used to dream about falling in love;
People said it couldn't happen 'cause I'm gay
and men don't do love, only toys and sex;
hasn't been, can't be, won't be any other way
for centuries, so what's so different now?
Besides, the Holy Books condemn
love relationships between two men;
it cannot exist (let alone last) in all conscience
and truth. Ah, but the romance and resilience
of youth will not be deterred from taking its due
as I discovered when I met you; electric shocks
seared through my body, scaring me as
your eyes bored into mine, seizing on thoughts
running wild in my brain, among them
a dream of falling in love although people say
it can't happen 'cause I'm gay. But now
your smile tells a different story, inviting me
to write my own history, reminding me I'm
my own man and love belongs to everyone
if they dare take a chance on themselves,
work at it as I worked on my doubts and fears
in the face of your beauty, our desires,
wanting to kiss your lips, tear off your clothes,
embrace a nakedness filling my mind's eye
with images of ecstasy, troubled heart set free;
O, joy! To be joined with you, find peace
and love, let them smother inhibitions, lies fed
by this tortured soul to an unforgiving heart
and make a start, at least, to live - by accepting
there is nothing to forgive, whatever they say
about us because we are two men and gay;
Yet, I turned away, my courage all but gone,
resolving to play safe though it mean

a lifetime spent alone. But you had other ideas
and caught up with me, took my arm,
swore you meant no harm, only that we should
spend some time together, take a chance
on each other, no matter we were strangers
contemplating potential dangers;
Don't friends justify means? Nor reason a need
when body and soul are screaming against
everything we've heard said (like gays
being better off dead...)

One by one, I let my fears drop away
in your eyes, like tears

BETTER LATE THAN NEVER

A winter cold near freezing;
city roads, country lanes
merging into a long nightmare;
Me, having no idea
where to go or what to do
for thinking about you;
Then I saw you standing there,
smiling and grey
like the winter sun, bursting
to re-appear, spread
a share of happiness for those
of us quick on the uptake,
seeking to fill our hearts with love
than stand by...
watch them break for the sake
of a bruised ego or two;
I didn't know what to say to you,
lips frozen and blue;
Besides, how to tell how sorry
for our quarrel - over
your being out and my being not
and neither of us willing
to compromise our points of view;
No surprise, we parted;
I watched you cross towards me
and caved in, you win;
it's time to tell the world and hold
my head up high;
Hand in hand, St Valentine's Day,
proud and gay

UP AGAINST IT

Two on Brighton prom
strolling along,
sure where we were going
and coming from...
for this world was ours,
yours and mine;
No one could touch us
or cause us pain.
love made us invincible;
Whatever do-gooders
might toss our way, we'd
have an answer for,
come what may. Ah, but
there were powerful
forces at play; gossiping
in corners, between
mobile texters, among
good neighbours
on smart patios, complete
strangers in heart-to-heart
bus queues, at pc screens,
over garden fences;
writing us off, damaging us
in parents' eyes,
giving even close friends
cause for doubt,
bosses excuses to find fault
till, exhausted, we must
be defeated? Well, almost.
But a tearful ghost
wearing a triangle saved us
with just one kiss

THEY

They said I should have stood up
to the bullies who tormented me
each day, that they'd have run away
had I not painted so vulnerable
a picture, central to adult
conjecture...

They said I shouldn't have given in
to the thug who demanded
I key in my P.I.N., draw my own
ransom from a cash machine
or he'd use a knife
on my spleen...

They said I'd be a fool to embark
on a gay lifestyle, it would
only bring me pain, a wasted life;
better to go straight, they said,
show the world you're a man,
take a wife...

They say life is all about survival
of the fittest - and who'll deny
that who laughs last, laughs long?
Well, I chose not to live a lie,
found love, am happy...
(That's wrong?)

Let the gossips have their say,
I'll live to laugh another day

THE ALPHABET CAT
(For Gary C.)

A cat sat on the mat
by the nursery door
but I never saw it move,
or heard it purr

It was there again
at the playground gate
as I tried to explain
why I was late

It was there too
on my first day at the office
watching me make tea,
load photocopiers

It was even there
when I took that holiday,
met my first love,
realised I'm gay

It's always there
on the same old mat
whenever I need
helping out

I wonder, will I ever
see it move, hear it purr,
find a cat on the mat
at Heaven's door?

SEEING IS BELIEVING

Fast asleep,
I did not hear the seventh stair
that would always creak
even when sly tiptoes trying
to sneak, unheard;
In a dream, as always, I stirred,
reaching out for you,
making-believe we hadn't parted
the way we did, lashing out
with cruel words, each wanting
to hurt the other more - it was
like committing suicide;
Your body pressed against mine,
this dream-self responding
eagerly, with passion, hot lips
relishing your tongue,
entering caverns of loneliness,
teasing me with a happiness
tossed aside that night we died.
What's this? A kiss, surely
meant to restore a lifeless heart,
let the blood course anew
through a body ready for a coffin,
forcing itself through each
pretend motion of everyday living,
taking where it can, giving
nothing in return, unable to feel
anything for yearning to taste
your mouth again, again?
My eyes flew open - and there
you were, no mere vision
of naked beauty but angel arms
holding me, our sexuality

awakening to the rising heat
of a true reality, no words
necessary

PAYBACK

Once, being gay was a crime;
not an easy time for us, cottages
among the few places we could
find people of a like mind for sex
of sorts...although no lift
to the soul, fumbling at a glory hole
or poking messages on a toilet roll
under a cottage wall, engaging shoe
for shoe, discovering what's to do,
sometime panicking, breaking out in
a cold sweat, running off, terrified
of everyday faces passing judgment,
demanding we each be punished
for our sin - again, again, again...
Now, thanks to Pride, humanity
recognized, places to go (bringing in
a pretty penny). Better days, yes,
where being gay pays - but payback
for many of us, in other ways

FOUND OUT

Eyes of gentle grey
telling a lie that's true,
seeing I'm gay

Lovers at play,
dark skies turning blue,
eyes of gentle grey

Some might say
I misperceived you
seeing I'm gay

A prayer on its way,
a loving word or two,
eyes of gentle grey

No pressure to stay
but I wanted to...
seeing I'm gay

Found myself that day
thanks to you,
eyes of gentle grey
seeing I'm gay

OUT IN THE COUNTRY

He asked me to dance
on the village green;
I jumped at the chance

Though neighbours askance
(some thought it obscene)
he asked me to dance

Forget all that token stuff
about poufs on-screen?
I jumped at the chance

Band playing by chance
our favourite tune,
he asked me to dance

Measuring every advance,
treasuring each joining-in;
I jumped at the chance

A subtle rush to ring-fence
(unsuitable for children?);
He asked me to dance,
I jumped at the chance

MY BEAUTIFUL LAUNDERETTE

My love declared he was leaving one day,
how he wished he'd never met me
and just - walked away;
For weeks, months, I roamed our streets
trying to forget about us,
cruising casual meets;
Then I met someone at the launderette
who had never been there before
and shared my soap powder;
We chatted on the wooden bench a while
and soon I was dying to tell him
how I loved his smile;
He and his girl were new to the city,
(puppy brown eyes beguiling,
letting me down gently?);
We'd meet there on a Sunday afternoon
but he never, once, mentioned
any girl again;
My ex-lover turned up again one day,
said he wished he'd never left me
and could we find a way?
I let him hug and kiss me but he guessed
it was too late, long before I confessed
my beautiful launderette

TOO SOON, TOO LATE

We walked by the sea
my true love and I...
dreaming, longing to be
twin doves in the sky

It had been a lovely day,
but twilight had fallen,
soon to take you away,
never mine again

Though years fly past
like those doves,
you're still the first, last
of all my loves

It wasn't a good time then
for two men

TURNING CORNERS

Told the world I'm gay,
overcame our fear;
lost, but found my way

Tired of running away,
spoke up loud and clear,
told the world I'm gay

On streets cold and grey,
sought a sunny corner;
lost, but found my way

Faces of wax and clay
cocked an ear,
told the world I'm gay

No matter what folks say,
it's good to be here;
lost, but found my way

Neighbours had a field day
(I even heard ma swear);
Told the world I'm gay;
lost, but found my way

GETTING PERSONAL

Over the garden fence, putting
the world to rights, tackling issues
that make no sense, whatever
some people might say,
like being gay;
Why should gay men be singled out
for persecution, advised we should not
raise children, told to consider
the ethics (so-called)
of social inclusion?
Who minds if a lesbian kisses
her partner on TV or walks out on
a man, willing to carry the can
for a marriage that's
broken down?
So why treat gay men differently
call their love a 'gross indecency' - or
shall we get grammatical (yes, let's)
and call it sodomy, according to
the dictionary?
Love is love and blessed be those
still sharing, no matter who or where;
Hate is hate and sad the soul
hell-bent on scoring
an own goal

ALTERNATIVE TRANSPORT

We chatted on a number ten,
smelt pouring rain,
felt young again...
chasing rainbows, pots of gold
and other fairy stories
gently told...
listening to a pitter-patter
on the roof - and
feeling safe;
We chuckled, exchanged a tale
or two and I felt comfortable
with you;
At your stop, I got off too
and we laughed at
getting wet...
walking on a street you thought
was mine, I thought
yours...
and a while before we hit
upon our comedy
of errors;
A second bus dried our clothes,
rumbling ifs and whys
of closet gays;
In his mirror, the driver winked,
saw better than either
of us...
how, even grown much older,
we'd struck gold on
a single-decker

BURIED TREASURE

He nearly always had a girl
at his side;
I could but adore him
from afar;
Sometimes, I'd stand beside him
at the bar,
we'd chat about this 'n' that
and all the while
it was all I could do to survive
his sweet smile...
without letting on how I felt,
my natural reserve
starting to melt like snow
in spring...
meant everything and nothing;
She'd play their song
on the juke-box for everyone
to enjoy - but me;
Later, they would leave together
and I would be alone,
ordering another beer (and more)
whinging how life
so unfair, others anxious to agree
but no idea why...
the words tumbling in a mad rush
like an avalanche,
burying us in my pain - till
I see him again

BAPTISM OF FIRE

Eyes closed, wishing my fear away,
the warmth of your skin, taste of your mouth,
touch of your hands eagerly exploring my sex,
making me wonder if it is me you see, desire,
or could it be just anyone lying here, available
to quench the fires of a passion I feel burning
us both up as we entwine, embrace, frantically;
Yet I cannot help but wonder if our desperation
is but a lie, a mere cover for the need to satisfy
an anxious physicality? It is you I want, crave,
long to enter me, join me to you as with a ring
I would thee wed but cannot so, instead, must be
content with this expression of a love unblessed
for society's native unwillingness to understand;
hurting me more, far more than throb and thrust,
throb and thrust, rising to a climax even as fear
continues to flood my mind, heart, every nuance
of my being here with you, wishing, wanting,
wondering...until, suddenly, we are done yet still
together, as one, drawing on each other's breath,
smell, a closeness as of children in the womb
listening to parents laughing, crying, singing, just
for being together, their love-making answer to
a prayer that we're wanted, loved, for who we are;
not afraid any more because I know now,
beyond all reasonable doubt, that you love me
as I love you and the world can take or leave us
as it will, lick of your tongue at the lobe of my ear
filling my senses, heart, soul, far, far more than
sexuality's responding to a glorious physicality,
acknowledging love's spirituality a truism,
this wetness of your tongue, a baptism

PRIDE AND JOY

Early one morning I walked with my love
into champagne-like bubbles of New Year,
cheery robins in turquoise skies above,
dew on a branch like a baby's first tear

Come noon we were strolling by the seashore,
children playing, couples laughing for joy
at being alive (who could ask for more,
asks each woman of man, each girl of boy?)

Twilight's embers found us in a garden,
branch left for dead, birds and babies asleep,
moon and stars as if begging our pardon,
behind dark clouds rarely able to peep

Hand in hand, towards a door shades of grey,
my love and I, unafraid to be gay

TELLING IT STRAIGHT

They told me being gay I would regret,
that I should take the conventional road
so family, friends, and people I met
wouldn't be offended or get tongue-tied

The onus was on me to realize
an obligation to society,
rendering to Caesar what is Caesar's
rather than courting impropriety

Having listened to all they had to say
and seen the way straight people carry on,
I beg to differ - it's not being gay
that's letting, dragging society down

Among the world's worst and saddest vices,
something said about stones and glasshouses

PART FOUR

WELCOME TO THE 21ˢᵗ CENTURY

WELCOME TO THE 21st CENTURY

Space probes in the galaxy,
harbingers of the Mars tourist;
24/7 banking on the Internet
(oops, beware a virus);
Violence on the streets, now
an everyday occurrence;
Drivers still using mobiles
at the wheel, refusing to believe
calling – or drinking - can kill.
(Besides, the chances are it will
be someone else who dies
and repentance always
goes down well with juries);
New legislation in the UK - to
make sure burglars are ok;
Meanwhile, people dying trying
to protect their own. Even so,
let's keep a sense of proportion,
a limit to self-defence
(or anarchy?) and what, pray,
pray, do our politicians have to say
about this? Not a lot…unless
an election round the next corner
then anything goes, if only to
pull the punters in on polling day
(or catch us out, as the case
may be). And how does religion
fit in with our daily lives?
Still preaching stories about peace
and loving our neighbours…
No matter, suspicion everywhere
we look – but how can we blame
our world leaders for that,
let alone bring them to book?

Dog fights dog, chases cat - and
always will, it's only natural,
like straight talking family values,
paying lip service to gay issues,
insisting women have equality
with men (except on the pay slip
they take home)

Oh, and God save the Economy!

Or, whatever it takes to keep up
appearances - no matter how many
arms and other shady dealings
going on in the name of liberation
and world fraternity

Welcome to the 21st century

NOT THE TEN O'CLOCK NEWS

Look at the world and despair
for all the pain and conflict here
and yet always be aware - of
goodness everywhere;
it doesn't get into newspapers
or on TV because goodness
isn't cool, doesn't send sales
soaring or boost ratings, hasn't
the drawing power of political
hot-spots, personal tragedy,
churches wrangling over gays
while Baghdad burns and Africa
struggles with HIV/AIDS
and even worse world leaders
than Sadaam Hussein are still
getting away with murder...
but, politically, remain far
too hard a nut to crack so better
to go for the softer option
and labour its merits to help win
an election, turning motivation
round (a kinder sound to ears
sick of the same old fairy story);
Truth is, goodness isn't always
good at all, of far less concern to
the world's Mandarins of Power
than what suit or robe to wear, the
rest of us meant to infer that our
best interests are on their agenda

So, down to you and me to prove
goodness lives, in peace and love

STAYING ALIVE

Like a snake it slithers inward,
a silent threat, making progress
all the time, its casual, everyday
camouflage blending perfectly
with our surroundings (no need,
surely, for any taking of soundings
for hidden warnings or heeding
secret signs, better focus on other
things, get on with our lives?)

Neither seen or heard, although
our senses start to prick the skin
at the predator's moving in on us,
trying to provoke an awareness,
the presence of danger, a crying
in the soul meant to warn,
but, too often, inciting anger
that - innocent - we should
be targeted for harm

Raise the alarm! Pull out all stops
and starts; a bringing together
of brave hearts, like minds,
confirming young David's aim,
wisdom of Solomon, inspiration
of Bible metaphor reworked in
everyday fable tucked away
in tabloids, radio, TV's appeal
to face facts, get real

Be a cancer in Eden's grass,
heaven endures...

CALIBAN'S SONG, 21st CENTURY

Stripped of integrity, deprived of dignity,
hung on a washing line to dry - then put
through the wringer again, again...
Mind, a mist, its damp heat soaks my sleep,
brings a welcome wetness though eyes
 stay dry, no matter how I long to weep...
for that daytime nightmare, made to share
with a world and its dog, that would stare
as if it were me cocking my leg up a tree;
No place to turn, words that can even begin
to explain the loneliness, desperation...
of a horror situation, its awful, nagging pain
for being misperceived, misunderstood,
sentenced to life, worse than any felon,
no clear recollection even of what I've done
to deserve (while deserve I may?) this...
being lost in hell's maze, no seeing ways
forward or back. Panic sets in, eagerly takes
cover in a corner of madness (easy enough
to mistake insanity for safety in the grip of
a sick anxiety to escape asylum's cutting
edge, eluded for years, too complex even for
a poet's imagination, let alone tears).Years on,
still counting the cost of dignity lost...
integrity stolen from me, trying (impotently?)
to hold my own. Battles lost, war - won?

A hollow victory some say, left to fight off
another day - till that sleep unbroken may
(finally) let us break free from a genetically
modified inhumanity

DEEP RIVER

A man by a river is always there,
usually fishing, sometimes drawing,
often gazing into the air as if watching
birds in flight only, invariably, there
are none in sight as the light on a face
all grizzled and worn (at first sight)
seems to shed all trace of care,
take on a saintly profile, beauty rare,
sublime, as heedless of time and place
as the river running by, emanating
centuries of loving, dreaming...
despairing of ever finding whatever
it may be we cannot cease seeking
though scared of naming, never weary
of hoping, trying to express however
we may - in the way we look, talk, take
walks alone, looking for someone...
half-convinced we expect to see no one
(if we do, what then?). A strange man,
people mutter and move on, few daring
to ask why he's always there by a river...
usually fishing, sometimes sketching
(often gazing into the air) a world full
of lost souls continuing to turn - on
the incapacity of a native curiosity
to translate into an oral perspicacity
leading to something better than this
mere passing on like a river...

TEA BAGS ON THE CENTRAL LINE

Forget sardines

Packed on the Tube like tea leaves
in a bag - without perforations;
Kettle on, steam coming out
of everyone's ears;
Dying for a brew. Instead, brewed up
for railway bosses...
to sip over their bonuses,
with digestives, one side chocolate,
(yummy) from the fridge - so not
dripping like some commuter dummy
mopping face, hands, neck,
wondering how the heck did I get
myself into this fine mess,
why don't I quit my job and go home,
rest up in the shade, treat myself
to a long, cold beer instead of being
brewed up here like a bad TV ad
meant to boost sales of tea, not
swap bags like me for the real thing,
high on the agenda for News at Ten
in the absence of fallout from
the political PR machine and what
about those raking in the harvest?
(No, not the slave labourer but
this spin doctor and fat cat - and what
are we supposed to make of that?);

I'll never be able to look a tea bag
in the eye again, even if a semblance
of normality should ever reconvene

Forget sardines

Note: Written during a heatwave in London (UK), August 2003.

BIRD BRAINS

Crow spread on the road
like a grubby smudge
in a busy diary;
Going about our business,
taking care, mobiles
at the ear;
Pouring over a crossword;
one across, two down,
a dead bird

WHO TALKS FOR THE TREES?

Two so-splendid trees stood tall
at the edge of a wood,
conspiring with song and laughter,
symphony and poetry
to run the gamut of serendipity;
all loves, hates, jealousies,
captured in shades of evergreen
on the costliest canvas seen
among the sweetest, finest blessings
of Nature, redefined by Man
in its own flawed image, redesigned
to suit an ailing humanity
along the lines of a well-meaning
insanity coursing the soul;
would-be giants grown tall,
sentinels of a civilization
protective of its own for want
of a wisdom of ages (found in
history's bloody pages?)
conspiring with song and laughter,
symphony and poetry
to stand tall among giant trees,
denying that Nature
knows best, mankind least, for all
its Grand Imagination touching
on salvation to defend a dereliction
of duty to save the woodlands
for next generations, rather give trees
up to property developers
for the sake of tax gatherers
giving them the eye and even if
the risen Jesus pause by
they'll not look up and see us,

hear a leafy wind whispering names
of all those struck down in youth or prime,
to a red and gold of flames among
glowing embers, no matter how many
11th Septembers

LONELY ROAD

Cats' eyes...
penetrating the darkness;
Darkness...
penetrating the soul;
Soul...
penetrating layers of time;
Time...
penetrating all identity;
Identity...
penetrating all pretence;
Pretence...
penetrating our dreams;
Dreams...
penetrating home truths;
Home truths...

Cat's eyes

WHOSE WAR?

Blood in the bedroom,
blood in the hall,
blood in the kitchen,
blood on every wall;
Bodies in the yard,
bodies in a field,
bodies in ditches
thinly concealed;
Tears at church services,
tears in class,
tears at the work place
slow to pass;
Terror in the air,
terror on a train,
terror all the time
closing in;
Prayers in the morning,
prayers at night,
sermons to the press
putting things – right?

Parliament, Congress,
Churches versus…?

SMOKESCREEN

Drifting, circling,
homing in
on us…
obscuring
deluding
confusing
the senses about
who we are
where we're going
what will become
of us…
drifting, circling,
closing in on
each other…
obscuring
deluding
confusing rights
and wrongs…
drifting, circling,
like buzzards
in a mist…
obscuring
deluding
confusing
who we are,
where we're going,
what will become
of us

Can't breathe

GETTING THERE

Walking down a street
in the dead of night
contemplating a good
night out;
No late birds winging,
drunken singing
or street lamps
working

Darkness

Moon, dozed off rather
than be taken to task
for stars snuffed out - by
God's own breath;
Come a roll of drums softly
on a summer breeze,
surely homing in
on me

Darkness

Seized by panic, a smell
of leather smothering
a yell, caught up in a bare
arm crueler than
barbed wire to a lamb
that's dying to break free,
frantically crying
for its mother

Darkness

Alone. Stumbling down
street after street at
dead of night – past being
scared . . .
Wanting, needing, desperate
to get home, wondering
if I'll ever feel safe
again?

Darkness

Years on, walking down
that same street, nor
by chance (friends to meet)
listening out;
Seems ages till cheery voices
begin turning the pages of
this, my darkness - then
O, bliss!

Light

EVERY POEM TELLS A STORY

Every poem tells a story...
about love, hate, shame, glory,
whatever inspires, lights
the fires of creativity, blind coals
in secret cavities of the soul
that now and then burst
into flames, lighting up the mind,
exposing the heart's needs,
its strengths and weaknesses
born of love, lust, hate, pain,
grieving for the world that it should
repeat its worst again and again,
leaving poor humanity to follow on
as best it can, put right
its wrongs, conveniently rewrite
the saddest songs of war,
disasters, wounds that will never
truly heal - with lines even
a paralysed heart can feel, though
it take a while to penetrate
its body armour, participate in the
latest United Nations resolution,
promises of aid on the way, more than
mere dreams fading as each day
turns into night, night into day, no one
(still) anything wiser to say
than - *Let's pray*. And where is God
in this world-spreading chaos,
saving a child dying of AIDS...?

Whose the power, where the glory
in poems that tell such stories?

ORDINARINESS

Clouds, a magic carpet ride
to exotic places;
Birdsong, awakening us to
a furthering of bath time
potential - rock star, jazz singer,
opera, whatever;
Grass, littered with daisies,
sunspots of memory;
Trees, waving leafy arms,
telling us off for things we've
done, forgotten, never
meant to happen;
A broken fence, urging us to
repair old friendships;
An empty chair, reminding us
of someone who'll never
sit there any more, words in
the air left unsaid;
Crisp, clean pillowcases, all
to ourselves;
Watching a damp patch on
the ceiling spread, fill the eye,
roll pictures in the head,
clouds passing by,
carrying us away from all this
self-conscious...

Ordinariness

NEMESIS
(For Linda M)

A stain on the wall
staring at me
accusingly;
Why do I let it stay,
not fetch a brush,
paint it away?
Oh, but I have tried
time and time
again...
but it glowers me,
devours me, the
awful stain;
Mindful of my own
mortality, it is my
only reality;
A ghost in my chair
(wonder why it's
there, me here?)
Oh, cruel indictment
on each of us;
Nemesis,
feeding on fate, even
among the world's
first families

SHELLING PEAS

Spilling out of their skins
as if anxious to be free,
like dreams, aspirations
for what cannot be

Heading for the colander
now the cooking pot,
a potpourri of mad desire
once tasted, never forgot

Big ones, small, sweet
on the tongue, an earthiness
teasing, letting us get
closer to godliness

if we dare, please,
shelling peas

NATURAL SELECTION

One particular branch of a tree
taps at my window
persistently

Anxious to be heard

A blackbird, too, among leafy
foliage, Nature's own
collage

Anxious to be heard

Until, one day, it came to me
how wrong (at best, naïve)
could I be?

Anxious for the world

Branch, bird, inviting me
to quit the comfort
of soap TV

Get real, like a tree

THE TABLE
(For Michaela)

Squat and shiny mutant turtle by a half open
window, chewing on memories more colourful
than weeds in the grass outside, recalling arms
reaching out; young wrists tapped for helping
themselves out of turn without even waiting to be
asked; assorted hairdos inviting comment and not
always receiving along lines preferred; bright eyes
looking here, there, everywhere but at what (or
whom) they really want to see; mouths kept busy
moving, even eating, when not picking at this 'n'
that, passing titbits to the cat rather than confess
to being on a diet or worse; ill chosen words
busy making more mess on the scaly surface than
years of ketchup and gravy that can never (quite)
be wiped out but remain like the sticky finger marks
of stubborn ghosts determined not to be forgotten
once this endless meal finished and everyone gone
our separate ways; sulking upstairs, walking off
a mood outside, taking on free washing-up therapy
in the kitchen, repositioning a chair at this very
table (the easier to watch TV). Perhaps we will
behave differently at the next meal; elbows off poor
turtle, conversation minimal, eyes fixed on his-her
food (must be a kinder place, surely, to hide?)

Or, maybe, we just died?

ON THE LIFE EXPECTANCY OF WEEDS
(For John Paul)

There is an ache in us, a weed grown tall,
no matter how hard we try to put it down;
It may be grief, relating to each petal
that ever fell, trod underfoot
as if never a flower at all;
It may be love, our hearts possessing,
found wanting or left undiscovered for
others to find while we're busy
chasing some map, piecemeal,
on a frantic treasure trail;
It may be hate, refusing to be put to rest
though we do our best to be adult about it,
kidding ourselves we're better than that,
can resist self-destruct;
It may be jealousy, a sense of inadequacy
for everyone going places, leaving us alone,
standing still, left to swallow
the bitterest pill of all;
Though on temporal fodder we feed,
no greater need than finding the right Word,
by which, secretly, we would have
our hidden selves be called...
risen above mere survival, select spawn
of a flawed humanity investigating (albeit
reluctantly, let's confess) the wider
implications of mortality

Thank goodness. Or how else to live, love,
dream, expect to enjoy poetry?

HOME THOUGHTS AROUND A TREE

Tree...
listening to bird songs,
leafing pages of our history,
its rights and wrongs.
Leaving, agree the swallows,
is best for all concerned;
Staying, argues a sparrow,
means lessons learned;
Grasshoppers chime in,
determined to have their say,
opinion divided, like this
slow death of day.
Sun, starting to go down,
moon ascending;
Twilight, giving way in tears
to sad worlds where
dreamers have softly trod, would
have stayed even,
returned to the galaxy all
that's given life, light,
peace in our time, heaven
in its sights. If only...
A whole new world in one tree;
see, hear its coming together
when natives, migrants, start
talking to each other;
Swallows, sparrow, grasshoppers,
hushed. Only a barn owl stirs.
Nothing, no one with any
answers

MONDAY, MONDAY

Monday morning, one eye
on a glorious dawning
through paper thin curtains
covering us like a shroud;
Hearts stopping, the ticking
of a bedside clock arousing
it to a semblance of beating,
rather like a bored child
tapping clean fingers - on
whatever happens along
to distract from the business
in hand of doing what's
expected, without so much as
any reward, let alone free
time off for good behaviour
from acting the epitome
of perfection, if only to impress
those who need to be
impressed, best impressions
leaving the rest struggling
to keep up and that won't do;
Have to show who's who,
stand up and be counted among
the better-than-we-are's,
prove our daily stars not so far
out after all, even if night
skies *are* more likely to shoot
us in the back, leave us
gibbering wrecks after playing
at sex and losing the game,
waking up with a killer hangover,
contemplating going to work
with abject terror, certain to be
gobbled up by some mean
office gossip machine;

Denial, retreat, playing those
you-can-tell-me-I-won't-tell's
at their own game, *may* have
something going for it I suppose,
beats unholy devotion to overtime
no one's paid, not to mention
swivel chairing gods of clay;
And for what - get laid, so drunk
we forget anyway?

.

Oh, Monday, Monday, just
GO AWAY

HEADBANGING

Graffiti on walls, across
urban sprawl

Magpies, at feeding
time

ON ALIENATION

Paintings on a gallery wall convey no sense,
no sense at all, simply make me feel a fool
because I'm supposed to be well educated,
applaud free expression, defend this artist's
gift for innovation, that sculptor's finer
perception of the world, this poet's mastery
of words, that prose interpretation of all we need
to shake us up, take us on a joyride, away from
all that's breaking up around us – like…
confidence in our leaders, respect for our elders,
relying on parents to teach us right from wrong.
No problem; just burn a CD and tell us it's
worth buying, put a few words together
and convince us it's clever, throw some paint
at a canvas or pile up some bricks and…
Before you know it, we're a generation of artists
in the making, potential just waiting to be keyed
into some base mentality like computer game
heroes for morons or trips to the Tate Modern
so we can play our part, imply we know what's
what about art and its love affair with life

Blank walls in a room, spinning us
like a humming top

Who's kidding whom - and how
to make them stop?

BLOOD AND STONES

Couldn't sleep, wouldn't sleep,
worrying myself sick about
everything from abortion to Iraq;
Asked my mother what I should do,
she told me to see my dad;
He merely sent me back to her, so I
sought out big brother instead;
Bro didn't have a clue, suggested
I talk to gran, who was busy
making marmalade, maybe I
could have a word with grandad?
Grandad was studying form
at the bookies, not to be disturbed,
so I sought out a friend, who needed
a shoulder to cry on, so I never
got a look in - although it's always
nice to know you're not the only one
slowly going insane for want
of someone to listen

WAITING FOR CHRISTMAS

Rain soaking shirt, jeans;
body responding freely,
face upturned, glad to be out
getting wet, mind distracted
from daily tensions;
Domestic crises, work targets
and assessments wreaking
havoc (with the best intentions)
stifling that very inspiration
meant to persuade, encourage,
leaves us feeling like flies
feeding on garbage left out
for the bin men, fodder for
stray cats, dogs, homeless folks;
Oh, we may have a job, home,
mortgage etcetera - but a life
to call our own? Some may
beg to differ, thinking through
the next day's staff rota
at supper, marking homework
once guests gone home (to
their beds); a thousand and one
working nights cramming
child heads, misting tired eyes,
tossing grave questions at us,
stirring up lies, half lies
meant to persuade, encourage,
leaves us feeling like flies
feeding on garbage left out
for the bin men to dispose,
counting the days till we get
to rubbish Santa Claus

CHRISTMAS TRUCE?

Sought a safe haven on Christmas Day
from family stuff, presents round a tree
giving the rein to how things should be,
denying what stares in each tinsel face;
A stranger in red mentioned such a place
where I might escape, find sanctuary,
even peace - away from all pretence at
burying home truths under layers of truce,
letting sweet carols on the ear replace
a harsher cacophony of lies, more lies,
accusation (and retribution?) for crimes
against the ego (never mind humanity)
in the daily round of sheer hypocrisy and
petty discrimination against whatever
points of view that can't, won't, shouldn't
always go with the flow in case we tread
on Someone's feelings, trigger into motion
a tedious chain reaction (even a violent
one) likely to go on and on for years,
spill more tears than cried for Judas
or lied about Christmas

So, where to go? I asked a jolly man in red
who started laughing, said to use some
commonsense and moved on, leaving me
for dead among piles of pretty wrapping,
more calls for a truce, plates of mince pies
and sausage rolls blind to a soul's fears,
deaf to its prayers

GOLD RUSH

Shadowy intersections
where the Devil meets its own;
Light, tripping over dark
like a drunken man, woman,
tumbling church steps...
or the whore in some persuasive
doorway, hands on hips,
a teasing smile licking the lips
of poker faces passing by,
pulses racing, quickening steps
like a ghost's hollow laughter
caught in a time warp on streets
littered with fool's gold
under a moon that's winking
at the world for its foibles though
without passing judgement,
unlike the cleric with half an eye
on heaven, the other...
looking to catch out we sleepers
tossing and turning,
spoilt for choices, yearning
for some peace of mind but
oh, so easily misled by brothers
and sisters of a kind...
seeking easy gold, seduced
by its glitter, reduced
to rummaging litter on streets
centuries old, same story
told at home, at school, teller
usually taken for a fool

A WINTER CANVAS

Straggly tree against a snowy sky,
robin redbreast in low key,
snowflakes like angels drifting by,
no more idea of what they're doing,
where they're going (or why)
than those of us down here, eagerly
lapping up the weather forecast
though for no particular reason than
everyone else will be doing much
the same thing so there's sense
of sorts in a camaraderie missing
in our everyday lives though friends,
family, do their best to assuage
spreading pains of loneliness,
poor self-esteem as we can't help
comparing ourselves with neighbours
who seem to be doing very nicely
while we're getting nowhere fast
like the poor weather forecaster
always trying to convince us better
days are just ahead, a robin singing
in winter, angels meant to explain;
why we're all running around God's
backyard like headless chickens,
world chasing its own tail after Peace
(its Holy Grail), politicians having to
make do with well-worn phrases
tried and tested out for no-substance
except election clout...

So what the heck is it all about
and - what's 'it'?

A CLASSIC IRRESOLUTION

Love strikes a classic pose,
signs it knows all I long to do,
where I seek to go...
a part of me I dare let few see,
the rest going by what I seem
to say, actions on display
for action's sake, decisions
I appear to make, trying to
right this wrong, that mistake,
appearing to be what I am not,
would rather lose, forget,
quit and gather seashells than
this walking on eggshells...
but too scared to walk away
from the daily ritual of swearing
to be good, strong, walk tall
and proud, vowing aloud
to earth and sun that I'm not
afraid to die before having
done all I would do, go where
I would go (wherever that be)
this part of me that would sleep
with young Apollo yet follow too
in the footsteps of Orpheus...

LINES ON DESPAIR

Like a killer in the night,
creeping up from behind;
throttles, stabs, whatever
other kind of torture
in mind to overcome us;
defeats, destroys, even
as we struggle, terrified,
to fight off the invisible,
the unexpected

Life but a finger's shadow
before our eyes, love too;
consumed by hate, deserving
better than this at the cruel
hands of a fate that promised
everything, now threatening
to cut us off with nothing,
all finer inspiration left
to brute infestation

One last lingering moment,
choices to be made - quit
a sorry world with integrity
(whatever the indignity)
or blunder, spent, through
a maze of uncertainty, wary
and afraid of half-shadows
in a long grey night, bent
on rewriting history

Despair, for our rising above
or interment of all we love...

AWAY FROM HOME

From a far-off land, they came, seeking
peace, hope, prosperity - probably
thought they'd made a good start
on a sprawling housing estate
in a country said by many to be great,
not least for being united against
injustice, hypocrisy, prejudice,
poverty. Tragically, it appears old habits
die hard, some discovering to their cost
how all that once shovelled the Great
into Britain now leaves it disunited;
a reverence for class, wealth - these are
(still) synonymous with breeding,
education, an ability to trace ancestors
to the Doomsday Book. Stiff upper lips
prevail; we shall see what we shall see,
mustn't blame a policy on immigration
entirely - or these people might get
the wrong idea, even suspect they're not
welcome here, especially (it must be
said) when some are being attacked,
abused and left for dead, others having
to settle for social handouts, begging
on our streets; more, too, doing their bit
for the economy, in dead-end
jobs, for blood money

So much for the 21st century...

MAKING WAVES

Storm raging across the sea,
lighting, thunder;
waves crashing mercilessly,
heads dragged under

Arms striving frantically
to keep death at bay;
O, for mother and trinity
to save the day!

Let the cruel sea have its say,
storm warning passed,
in its own time and way
bring peace at last

Swim or drown, making
waves of our own

ALL THE WRONG PIECES

Anarchy in bus queues;
Assault-by-default
on rush hour trains

Death on the roads;
Date rape in bars;
Gun law on the streets

Perverts coasting;
Hypocrites anxiously taking
Communion

Disabled access leaving
much to be desired;
Gays, blasted

People in self-imposed
segregation making the most
of whatever legislation

Society's jigsaw parts
little more than thoughtlessly
discarded litter

UNDER PRESSURE

Can't sleep well at night for worrying
about this, fretting about that, wondering
how to pay mortgage, rent, phone bill,
credit card debts, a Council Tax that
(like TV licensing) deserves the axe
for all the positive results we see after
forking out each year, not even sure we
can afford anti-depressants any more,
prescription charges going up to keep
the Treasury happy; no wonder the patient
struggling to survive, make ends meet
in western societies that could learn a lot
from Third World counterparts where,
in spite of civil wars, poverty, famine,
HIV/AIDS, same corruption in high places,
a tribal spirit persists, keeping the best
oral traditions alive, lessons for the world
today; come what may, playing their part,
giving heart to even the poorest places
where the most always have least, the least
deserving doing very nicely, watering
money trees in glasshouses Mother Church
will have (discreetly) blessed, making
capital out of charity, hand over fist...

WHEN THE WIND BLOWS

A north wind penetrating within,
purging the soul, tearing the skin
from a body staring ruin in the face
and no way back to the way
things were but a leaf or flower
away, driven to choose this track
or else no chance of winning;
Hope fading, risk losing
everything

Blows the wind cruelly, tears freezing
on a face turned to heaven, seeking
aid, mercy, grace, forgiveness
for the error of our ways, judgements
cast in stone to boost an ego
begging superiority over erstwhile
minorities, teeth showing whiter
than the smile on a hungry tiger
selecting priorities

Persevere. Let fear do its worst,
we shall endure, the sun shine
in our faces again, belie the damage
of acid rain, camouflage our pain
under a blank sheet of paper
signifying nothing, signing us up
for whatever the world may say
we must feel, no matter what's
just or real

An echo, like wolves howling,
of cash druggies prowling...

A GAY BASHING

I found him late at night,
bleeding in a gutter, near dead,
his fine features an ugly sight,
white shirt turning red;
I called an ambulance, did all I could
to comfort, help ease his pain
but it seemed a long time coming
and he but hardly breathing
as I struggled to speak,
keep him awake, scared
lest he close his eyes and it might
well be the last time he would
hear a voice, feel its warmth
spread over him like my coat;
I offered a prayer, could not bear
that he should leave this life
a victim of ignorance and hate
although a part of me knew
it was already too late - for them
as much as him - given the world
as it is today, paying lip service
to issues gay while, behind
a public front of liberality,
cheering for the sheer bestiality
of a criminality seen as justified
because gays are scum, deserve
no better, no matter how (supposedly)
we share a common humanity...
yet, in a sea of sirens, discovering
new strength in straws

ANNUAL REPORT

Born to lead, fulfil, unite;
invariably, though, dividing,
losing sight of how many
chosen to fight on one side
rather than chance losing face,
faith in an interpretation of
rights and wrongs pointing
clearly to a strategy - for
victory over mortality

Come to bring peace, hope;
Invariably, though, screws up
at practically every turn for
each well-meant move taken,
every word preached ringing
with sincerity (Truth's old
enemy) better placed than
any to take a dove's eye
view of our morality

Pigeon-holed by history,
shaped by the eternal mystery
of Creation, each to our own
interpretation, verification
according to temporal needs
and desires, lighting the fires
of spirituality - a common
humanity or personal gain,
as the case may be

Christianity, Islam, whatever,
can do better, must try harder

THE WORLD TODAY

TRUTH OR DARE?

Mirror on the wall,
truth or dare?
Exposing us all

Mind, heart, soul
laid bare;
mirror on the wall

Pride before a fall
without a care,
exposing us all

Hurt of a Jekyll
in Hyde's lair;
mirror on the wall

Let free voices call
but turn a deaf ear,
exposing us all?

Echoes in the hall,
any listener can hear;
Mirror on the wall,
exposing us all

WHO'S COUNTING THE PETALS?

Floods here, drought there, disease, swollen bellies...
Refugees from civil wars pleading aid;
Terror taking place on our own TVs;
men, women, children, taught to be afraid

So what are the world's governments doing?
All they can, we're expected to believe;
So why tragic images we're seeing
of a world wearing its heart on its sleeve?

Where horror hits hardest, a hurt laid bare;
Beyond headlines, inconceivable pain;
Flowers at gravesides, each petal a tear
for those men, women, children moving on

Cash flowing freely for wars, elections
(Business politics for generations)

A CARER'S SONG

How many times must we reach for the stars,
wish the pull of earth's gravity away?
How many years wipe someone else's tears
and no one even ask if we're okay?

How many times must we watch on TV
proof of Man's inhumanity to Man,
a tear in the eye as we sip coffee,
sighing as we reach for the telephone?

How many times must we try to advise,
only to have kind words thrown back at us?
How many years live someone else's lies,
our own feelings baggage in a suitcase?

Come a day, freed to set life's burden down,
pray someone, for us, let a candle burn

WHATEVER HAPPENED TO GOOD NEWS?

Some say death is but a gentle sleeping,
gone in pursuit of such beautiful dreams
that awakening at a new dawning
finds a far better world than now it seems

Looking around at the world as it is,
who can't say they don't want to run away
from terror on the streets and drunk drivers
throwing the dice at justice every day?

Rarely does the penalty fit the crime
or a victim get as fair a hearing
as the perpetrators playing for time
with tales to keep news editors cheering

Ah, let's put aside all we see, hear, read...
long enough to concede a life that's GOOD

BANGLADESH, 2004

Sewage everywhere,
ugly tide of homelessness,
disease a growing fear

Faces weeping despair,
global rise of helplessness;
sewage everywhere

Eyes a widening stare,
at Nature's senselessness;
disease a growing fear

Mouths sucking in air
denied earth's fruitfulness;
sewage everywhere

Watching people suffer
on wide multi-channel TVs;
disease a growing fear

Tragedy enough to scare
us out of our western-ness?
Sewage everywhere,
disease a growing fear

SILENT WITNESS, SUDAN 2004

One by one, see them fall in the sand,
women, children, tears run dry;
skeletons of war in a savaged land

Men and boys killed where they stand,
only God asking why?
One by one, see them fall in the sand

Infants born into the palm of a hand;
no one hears them cry;
skeletons of war in a savaged land

Hunger, want, pain, a despairing band
of pilgrims at the altar of a lie;
one by one, see them fall in the sand

The world looks on, would lend a hand
though many ask, why even try?
Skeletons of war in a savaged land

Heaven unmasked, Death unmanned,
Life, like Love, a proud if muted cry;
one by one, see them fall in the sand,
skeletons of war in a savaged land

TEARS OF THE SUN

Falling, tears of the sun
on God's good earth;
a weeping never done

For each man, woman
world-weary since birth,
falling, tears of the sun

For refugees on the run
yearning home and hearth,
a weeping never done

Civil wars, AIDS, famine,
of lonely prayers a dearth;
falling, tears of the sun

Terror, the new religion
at this 21st century's birth,
a weeping never done

For the people's politician
a quickening of stale breath;
Falling, tears of the sun,
a weeping never done

THE POLITICS OF CAIN

Weapons of mass destruction
(sexed-up for good measure?);
the politics of Cain

Death, maiming, division
over Earth's darkest treasure;
weapons of mass destruction

Harvest of arms provision
gathered at leisure;
the politics of Cain

One body of persecution
but exchanged for another?
Weapons of mass destruction

Looting, killing, in desperation
and worse yet to weather
the politics of Cain

Brave, indeed, the politician
tugging at its 'special' tether;
Weapons of mass destruction,
the politics of Cain

THIRD WORLD WAR

Fight against terror
spreading like a virus;
Third World War

Self-styled saviour
in the White House
fight against terror

Carnage and horror
selling newspapers;
Third World War

Wooden spoon stirrer
in Parliament capers'
fight against terror

All hail the martyr!
Fundamental chorus,
Third World War

Victim and perpetrator,
counting our losses;
Fight against terror,
Third World War

WAR OF THE WORLDS

For nature's riches we lust,
some costly battles won,
and whose laugh the longest?

To life's battlefield, needs must
all fighting men and women;
for nature's riches we lust

In our faiths we put our trust,
hear an echoing *Amen*...
and whose laugh the longest?

Time, carrying us so far so fast;
now spears, now lasers gain;
For nature's riches we lust

All smiles at a harvest feast
(no thanks to acid rain)
and whose laugh the longest?

Needing the most, getting least;
live ghosts groaning in pain;
For nature's riches we lust
and whose laugh the longest?

WINDS OF THE DAY

Free or thrall,
live as we choose;
Our call?

Rise or fall,
win (yet still lose)
free or thrall

No crystal ball
deciding our dues;
our call

Only the soul
its own truth knows;
(Free or thrall?)

In breeze or squall,
as the mind blows...
Our call

Ugly, beautiful
as a day comes, goes;
Free or thrall?
Our call

LAMENT FOR A GRASSHOPPER
(For Keith)

Once I heard a grasshopper sing,
heard the dawn chorus...
where now trucks thundering

I have heard bluebells ring
sweet sounds of silence;
Once I heard a grasshopper sing

I saw a stream, twisting, turning,
haunted by otters...
where now trucks thundering

I have watched birds mating
in leafy trees;
Once I heard a grasshopper sing

There used to be a graceful flying
of kingfishers...
where now trucks thundering

Needs must, called 'progress'
through the centuries;
Once I heard a grasshopper sing
where now trucks thundering

WHERE DID ALL THE BABY OTTERS GO?

There was a stream that ran down a mountain
through this gutted forest, that daisy field,
joined sewage spilling without correction
over banks where once baby otters played

As men and women challenged the mountain,
would feed also at heaven's angry breast,
so its life-giving milk turned to poison,
killing us off like the otters, God rest...

The snows of the mountain slowly melted,
flooding forests, fields, humankind and beast;
city folks too, slowly forced to admit
their share of the blame neither all nor least

Who deserves to survive global warming,
greedy for oil - car, our comfort and king?

SUB SEVEN TROJAN HORSE

Realism, an anathema
to every dreamer-poet,
feet on terra

Unrequited lover,
victim of self-deceit;
Realism, an anathema

Unhappy key worker
stays, longing to quit,
feet on terra

Abused son, daughter,
paying dearly for it;
Realism, an anathema

No way to beat terror
by closing the mind to it;
feet on terra

Crisis commuter,
crossword half complete;
Realism, an anathema;
feet on terra

ASYLUM

Love, where the heart is,
our history in the making,
building better countries

Life, with new neighbours,
old enmities forsaking;
Love, where the heart is

On us, the onus of peace,
each new dawn breaking,
building better countries

Our origins, surely, precious
embers for the raking;
Love, where the heart is

Learning to be at ease,
same dreams for the taking,
building better countries

Home, where we choose,
(differences equably debating?);
Love, where the heart is
building better countries

SPELLING IT OUT

Some people tell me
(who know better?)
HIV+ spells misery

Global object of pity
like a leper,
some people tell me

Others say despairingly,
since AIDS a killer,
HIV+ spells misery

Ultimate degeneracy,
self before natural order,
some people tell me

Losing faith in society
as father or mother,
HIV+ spells misery

Fighting hypocrisy,
living truthfully,
some people tell me
HIV+ spells misery

S-WORD IN THE SHEATH

Death is but a word,
a poet's metaphor,
sheath for a sword

A dark sound heard
at the inner ear,
death is but a word

Its presence assured,
meaning obscure,
sheath for a sword

A threat endured,
challenge clear,
death is but a word

Our fear abjured,
by Love's own favour,
sheath for a sword

Its blade removed
draws kisses in the air;
Death is but a word,
sheath for a sword

ON TAKING RESPONSIBILITY

We broke the pot,
a Guardian Angel cries;
we mend it?

Birthdays forgot,
the old beggar dies;
We broke the pot

Loyalty split,
God knows we tried;
we mend it?

Where peace could not
get the better of pride,
we broke the pot

To each our lot,
a cutting of life's thread;
we mend it?

Marking the spot
where Eden gone to seed;
We broke the pot,
we mend it

KNOWLEDGE OF CANNIBALS

We know the time must come when we will die
but when it does, what last moves do we make?
Do we pray, weep, or simply say goodbye
to the few we have loved for love's own sake?

Dying, will some distant God now restore
peace of mind, the innocence of a child,
or must we writhe in pain at Heaven's door
pay the full price for being of this world?

What is repentance and what does it prove
but a desperation to be rescued
from an eternity without light, love,
freefall in a hell by our own sins spewed?

Tell me, do we defy (whose?) forgiveness,
persist in feeding on our own darkness?

A PRISONER'S SONG

In the beginning, a womb's blind charade
kept me guessing about being outside;
Discovered, the cruelties of childhood
then living with maturity's dark side

In the womb, I needed no excuses;
By the world's light, I was almost blinded;
As a child, I learned about secrets, lies;
In society's swim, I all but drowned

I have never heard what I've yearned to hear,
returned (sincerely) words we're taught to say,
perceiving the world as a prisoner...
though entitled to equal rights of way

In the end, there's only myself to blame
for failing to call my warders by name

SUMMONED BY GHOSTS

Come a late hour's whim, witness home hills turn
to silver ghosts, shades of midnight's children
playing with stars, prisoners of the moon,
unable to sleep, anxious for the dawn

Above, chance to watch an owl's graceful flight,
see it circle, swoop, soar, but can only
guess at its prey - victim too of a night
no friend to the vulnerable, lonely...

I have wandered, asked questions of shadows
mocking me, teasing me with solutions
chasing grey rabbits across dark meadows,
party to a sad mind's convolutions

At last, hills and sky hosting a new day,
ever hopeful of keeping ghosts at bay

DAGGERS IN THE HEART

I'll be your friend, a child told an old man
but the old man shook his grey head, sighing;
the child took two careworn hands in his own,
wondered why the rheumy eyes were crying

I can't be your friend said the old man gently,
some people will get the wrong idea;
they'll be looking at you, looking at me
and it will be the worse for us, I fear

I must be on my way said the old man,
I've been sitting on this bench far too long;
Go child and have fun, as much as you can,
it doesn't last, innocence, being young...

The child ran off, puzzled at catching gran
throwing daggers at the kindly old man

DIVIDED WE FALL

Subtle divisions,
tablets of stone;
our religions

Contradictions
every one;
subtle divisions

Good Samaritans
to the bone,
our religions?

Pulpit re-unions
for God's lesson;
subtle divisions

To the politicians,
a daughter, son,
our religions

Holy constitutions,
bloodily written;
Subtle divisions,
our religions

TRIUMPHANT VOICES

Through terror strike fear
into the heart,
we shall persevere

Listen, and we can hear
a pop song start...
though terror strike fear

Here, there, everywhere,
lives torn apart;
we shall persevere

Listen, young voices clear;
we play our part...
though terror strike fear

Pity the poor slaves to war
losing out;
we shall persevere

No matter the arms dealer
politicking clout;
Though terror strike fear,
we shall persevere

THE WORLD TODAY

The world today is full of pain and fear,
guns on the street, in the playground, the park;
drugs, like body bags lying here and there,
knives sticking in the back at home, work

Where the war on terror taking its toll,
people half afraid of their own shadows;
fanatics failing to make us look small
but no letting up on suicide bombers

Newspapers at breakfast turn the stomach;
Need pills to keep going, more to aid sleep;
No one seems to care about very much
but making money, getting into debt

The world today is full of pain and fear...
but there's love too - and glad I am I'm here

PART 5

A FEELING FOR THE QUICKNESS OF TIME

A FEELING FOR THE QUICKNESS OF TIME

Yesterday gone, today soon done,
tomorrow already on the run
from mindless shadows toying
with unkind thoughts, like
a child sent to bed early, a lesson
to be learned but, instead,
filling the head with lies, half lies
and few home truths getting
a look in, determined to feel hard
done by, resolved not to cry
(would rather die than let anyone
see how much it hurts to be
missing TV denied pc games,
nothing to do but call people
names); could read a book but who
wants to do that? And they've
taken the walkman away too, talk
about getting even, pulling
rank. Being a kid's a thankless
affair, just wait till I'm older,
I'll show 'em what's what, high
time they learned what life's
all about - too short to fuss about
being late home, although
(fair enough) should have used
the mobile to say so - but
what the heck? Got home okay
eventually, didn't I? (Parents,
who'd have 'em?). Ranting and raving
at a window, watching the sun
die away, listening for voices used
to hearing say 'don't, can't
shouldn't, mustn't, old enough to

know better' – shows they care
I suppose, and an early night's not
the end of the world in anyone's
language even if, like the mantel clock,
we're loath to acknowledge a fault,
tailoring time's cloth to suit the parts
we play; child grown-ups getting
a life, demanding a real say in how
our stage be set - not 'one day perhaps'
but a resounding yes, NOW

SWEET BIRD OF YOUTH

I grow old
yet not cold
for the sun is warm
and so is the rain
that makes me young
again, again,
my blood run hot
for all I have
than have not;
For the past is gone
and the future…
who knows?
But the present,
the *present* is mine
and I fly with
swallows

CHARGING UP FOR CHANGE
(For Barry & Diane)

O, those formal, frumpy fifties!
What I remember best...
are TV announcers in evening dress
(even in the afternoon)
being glued to the radio (hangover
from wartime) when not letting
Bronco, Cheyenne, Wagon Train
mythicize the American West;
Then along came skiffle;
Rock 'n'roll began to take root;
Juke Box Jury woke us up
from days of ballroom dancing
to new frontiers of Disco,
(forget the Lone Ranger and Tonto);
Mods and rockers hit the headlines,
girls starting to adapt their hemlines
to more than simply fashion,
boys discovering drainpipe trousers
and winkle-picker shoes;
Off 'n' away with post-war blues!
Along came Z-cars, elbowing
out Dixon of Dock Green (doomed
to bite the dust along with Bronco
and the rest) - the sixties taking over,
Beatlemania on a par with religion
and politics fair game for any Sister
or Brother free, supposedly,
to have a mind of their own...

From frumpy fifties to swinging
heaven – or wistful imagination?

A QUESTION OF TIMING

Doors flinging and slamming,
windows opening, closing,
streets stretching, bending;
Children born and growing,
parents coming, going,
working at living,
trying to make out they won't
mind dying so long as the
timing's - what, right?
Earth flung, heaped and piling,
buds opening, closing,
footpaths stretching, bending;
Chicks nesting and growing,
parents coming, going,
working at living,
trying to make out they won't
mind them flying so long as
the timing's - what, right?
More flinging and slamming,
mouths opening, closing,
legs stretching, bending;
Love born and growing,
hate coming, going,
working at praying,
trying to make out it doesn't
mind dying so long as the
timing's - what, right?

KILLING TIME

Rushing to the door,
flicking through the post,
anxious for a franking,
means the most;
Bills, bills, junk mail,
postcard from auntie Mary
on a coach tour
in Tuscany;
Need a holiday, promised
the family - fat chance while
faced with daily
misery;
Operation cancelled twice,
shortage of staff, call on beds,
must get it right, no
mistakes;
A letter? Hope, keeping body
and soul together, wrestles with
a stomach churning over,
runs for cover;
Putting on a face
(and some favourite CDs)
praying the next post will
bring better news

Goes the day slowly, no
second delivery

DIANA

Goddess of the moon, quiet and shy
but a stubborn streak (never weak);
Radiating a love she sought in others,
empathy with fellow sufferers;
Found herself less than a refugee
in Establishment territory;
Rose above arrogance, deception,
betrayal of the worst conception;
Learned to give as good as she got
and more besides, made enemies;
No flawless icon, a woman of stature
unafraid to embrace human nature...
Good, bad, dark, light, shades between,
all flowering humanity, roots of pain;
Her passing, victim of conspiracy
or legend, centuries in the making?
Her legacy, a smile that inspired,
fired the hearts of millions

Great is Diana of the Ephesians

HOLLYWOOD BOULEVARD

Walked with Death one
afternoon, watery sun
and a misty rain;
Man, woman, I couldn't
tell - Humphrey Bogart
or Lauren Bacall?
Better than any movie,
the suspense really
getting to me;
And where would I be
by the end of the day?
Strained to hear...
what my companion had
to say about it, though
abysmally scripted;
Caught words like fate,
jealousy, love, hate,
sounding as trite
as ma's plastic mac worn
to fend off a heavy
summer storm;
Only, no storm broke
nor did Death call me out
by name,
making do with barely
disguised threats
and innuendo;
Should I take the bait?
Oh, I thought I might
but - no;
Rather, I quickened my
step, widening the gap
between us...

where I could hardly see
hand in front of face
for tears...
and a glaring sun, already
killing off mist, rain,
and my worst fears

BIRDWATCHING

Death
is an egg
fallen from its nest
to the ground

Splat

Sibling
surviving
to hatch and test
its voice

Ah

Life experiences
of a child

ALCOHOLIC ANONYMOUS

A stranger, drowning in a sea of faces,
not a smile to cling to, no hint of caring
in dead eyes staring straight ahead,
waves of indifference crashing on me,
putting me down, hauling me up, only
to toss me back with all the contempt
of a fisherman for minnows competing
for Angler of the Year, a title bringing
fame and beer (for years) at the local pub
where I used to drink my fill; too often
some would say - and how I find myself
this way, a stranger among old friends;
Now, a fish out of water gasping for air;
Now, clinging for dear life to a can
of beer, almost past caring any more,
glad to let myself fall though unwilling
to take you with me (you deserve better)
flailing like a half-dead fish left to its own
meagre devices. May survive, may not,
each to our own choices, whether it be
win, lose, drift along woebegone, food
for fishes or some amateur fisherman
casting a line from posterity's shelf,
shades of myself as once I was before
I went looking for more (in a can of beer)
seeking adventure, bored with the sheer
predictability of domesticity, dead-end job
a hook reeling me into limbo, serving up
this zombie on a plate that's a street
I used to walk, head high, pausing to chat
now and then with friends who appear to
have forgotten who I am so I don't even try
to catch their eye any more, doesn't come

as any surprise any more, can't even think
beyond the next (just one more...) drink,
avoiding local bars in case someone sees

TREADING THE BOARDS

For all the hours, years
of laughter, tears, where's
the gain? Blind strokes of joy
against a backcloth of pain;
And when the show is done,
what then - more of the same?
Acting out names, playing up
to dreams, all those taking part
deserving accolades, no matter
crooked trees, convincing lies
written into cartoons by authors
anxious to avoid court cases;
Better by far, though, we go
in disguise for not all bears
hunt among trees - crooked
or otherwise

Calling on all writers, actors
and scenery painters...

DEAR PM

Though whomsoever may read this letter
think it perverse I write in free verse,
it seems appropriate enough to me, given
the mess we're making of this century
so far; I mean, should we pat ourselves
on the back for making our citizens
of a better tomorrow pay through the nose
for it - when who more likely to reap the
benefit than us? As for making war on any
country far less equipped than ours simply
because it presents a *potential* threat...
what do we *really* think of that? It's down
to politics of course and getting even for
September 11, no matter who else lives
or dies and, of course, it has nothing to do
with oil revenues. So we live in a world
stalked by terror, who's to blame? Do we
pick a name, any name, put a price on its
head, even bring a pack of cards into play,
anything to distract attention from matters
of political persuasion that defy invention,
never mind any intervention from ordinary
men and women or this religion and that,
all vying for prime time TV, or better still,
a say on News At Ten? What's up with us,
dear PM, if we can't see wood for trees
any more (and where have all *they* gone?);
Internet is here, a valuable tool, means
of communication the world over - so how
about chatting with a next door neighbour
one of these days, take a break from surfing
cyberspace? Try it, at least, might see how
reality bytes at the mention of a gay priest,

so-called 'designer babies' to save lives,
those whose time fallen into decay forced to
humiliate themselves trying for the right
to die with dignity even if the Human Rights
lot can't bring themselves to agree. Worse,
how about gays adopting a kid? How crude!
Everyone knows you have to be dead straight
to bring love into the world. And, yes, it's a
dangerous place, we must be cautious, but
does it help to be kind to burglars? As for this
global warming, what's it all about and GM
food – what on earth is that, where's the damn
debate? It can't hurt to try, at least, to educate
Joe Public (not to mention, Josephine) though
our leaders seem to think too much knowledge
will flummox, better just back the favourite
at the ballot box. And what about zoos?
I sometimes wonder about those and who's
to say we won't end up in one, endangered
species every one of us daring to have
minds of our own, vote with our feet, make
our voices heard in country lane, High Street,
join together - no matter colour, creed, sex,
sexuality, put an end to senseless divisions
for the sake of personal ambitions, being seen
to be heading for the top, no cause to brake;
Surely, we should think this through? It's not,
what I want for the 21st century - do you?
To a kinder self, let's be true, less prejudice
and sheer hypocrisy to show for it.

Signed, A people's poet

HOW LONG BEFORE THE NEXT BUS?

Blood on the pavement where a body lay
and, later, someone knelt to pray for the soul
of a young person struck down long before
their time; senseless crime, harsh indictment
of a society more likely to pass by on the other
side than come to anyone's aid being attacked
for the sake of a few quid to buy acid, coke,
crack, designer gear, the chances are because
some in-crowd says it's 'cool' to look good,
act big enough to scare old ladies into having
heart attacks, snatch a blind man's stick for a
(sick) joke. Ah, but some folks may fight back,
end up dead (not so cool, eh, with a price on
the head?). Years later, and pain still tearing
at society's flimsy fabric, ripping it as hate did
a young person's jacket whose blood at that
bus stop tells its own tragedy, plaque meant as
a memorial as likely as not serving to recall the
vainglory of a fraternity never properly brought
to book, maybe never will be, so we can't even
walk down a street any more without tasting
a fear in the mouth that's perverting the course
of justice, harmony, in a world likely to stab us
in the back any time for how we seem; white,
black… no matter colour, creed, sex or sexuality,
easy targets for the perversity of thugs on a street
that could easily be mine or yours - our mother,
father, sister, brother or best mate saying prayers
for us left waiting, anxiously, for the next bus

YES, WHAT?
(For Finola)

If I'd said this, or that,
said - what?
If I'd done this, or that,
done - what?
Tortured souls crying out
their guilt, left
hanging in some limbo
to - rot?
What good purpose, that?
None.
We cannot (ever) change
what's done,
bring back loved ones
long - gone?
No, but here in the heart,
forever
willing us to live again,
move on;
Nothing said or done then
would - what?
Have eased whose pain,
whose guilt?
Choices, rarely plain, but
ours alone
will take us here, there,
where?
No one to blame having
chosen - wrong?
Who's to say, play judge
and jury?
Enough, surely, to be...
what, exactly?

LEFTOVER PIE

Dawn, slitting windows like laser beams,
forcing open eyes bent on shutting out
the world. Drawing breath, steeling limbs
for roll-call, trying to reassure troubled
mind, heart, that this is no kick restart
for failed hopes, living nightmares - but
a new beginning, risen on a crest of birds
singing, carried on gentle waves of spring,
sleeping seeds sure to wake, grow, bloom,
fill the eye with colour, let us find our way
once more around words of terror imposed
like blots on the landscape - here, there,
wherever we look everyone making out
we had better get used to it

Earth a closed book to all but Everyman,
written and rewritten by judges (no jury),
politicians (same old story) and those
closer to God than we, claiming to be in
the know, blaming the world for its own
damnation, marking out the boundaries for
our salvation according to whatever cut
and cloth of this congregation or that;
As for those who choose to go our own
way than let the politics of power bring
the world to its knees – we may suppose
(whose?) God will have the final say,
refuse to rescue us as we lie in our beds
ripped to shreds by laser beams?

Leftover dreams of love and peace, daring us
try for pie-in-the-sky

LINES ON TIME

Time, a fickle friend
though her gifts be free,
with us till no-end

As broken lives we try to mend,
we press on hopefully;
Time, a fickle friend

Rely on Time, her love to lend
though often mixed with pity,
with us till no-end

Life with love may play 'Pretend'
yet each day pass joyfully;
Time, a fickle friend

Precious minutes, hours, confound
long months, years, tearfully...
with us till no-end

May heaven its angels send
across the killing fields of eternity;
Time, a fickle friend,
with us till no-end

A MATTER OF TIME

There's a long road that winds
past the cemetery – and sometimes
I'd take a shortcut...
by graves, flowers, yew trees,
headstones wiped clean – or left
to gather weeds, moss;
I'd find myself wondering
about this thing called Death,
so near, so far;
Should I be scared of or resigned
to its appalling inevitability,
on a high even...
since the whistle on my lips
is real, no breeze in sentinel trees
whispering in the ear?
Shriek of a starling's return
to the nest, magpie come and gone,
done its worst;
Flower heads, like ghostly eyes,
watch my every move, smiling
at me as I hurry along...
opening their hearts to a sun
that means them well, no reason to
suspect nightfall...
or anything other than a helping
hand from Mother Nature to preserve,
keep safe, petal, stem, root...
and if wind or rain our pleasure
displace, plenty others eager to take
their place;
Relieved to reach the tall iron gate,
giving death behind me barely
a thought - but can't help

wondering, walking down a street,
why a red rose in the gutter
should suddenly matter?

POPPIES FOR FEARS

In two world wars, and conflicts since, they died
for love of country, freedom and their own;
Shells, mortars, bullets and bombs they defied
so we may reap the rewards they have sown

Let's remember those who never came back,
sitting comfortably watching TV;
Somme, Dunkirk, Korea, Falklands, Iraq...
(So much for the lessons of history!)

The wounded, too, deserve our thanks and pride,
some forgotten, left but to fade away
in pain, loneliness, no one at their side
as fought with them so bravely, won the day

Poppies for remembrance, prayers, shedding tears
and - world peace to put an end to our fears?

SHOT IN BLACK AND WHITE

The earth was white, the sky black,
one midnight in mid-winter
when I looked out of my window
and saw a light snow falling,
thought I head an owl calling...
(But, no, mistaken, surely?)

Then I saw it, a silvery bird gliding
phantom-like through this curtain
of frozen rain like an image sewn
into a lace tablecloth that graced
our table, years ago, when we
ate as a family...

No family now, only a scattering
of memories like winter snow
piling on a branch by my window,
higher even than regrets that
eyes glaring back at me wilfully
deny - or do they lie?

Gone, the owl now, its beauty
but a passing moment...
like time spent at mealtimes
when wrong was wrong
and right was right, the world
coloured black and white

The wind is up. A blizzard throws
an angry net over glaring traffic
on the night shift, testing the weary
and faint hearted (re-asserting
an omnipresence lest we become
too complacent?)

Owl, shot by a night lens for a BBC
documentary, last seen returning
to its own. Surreal, any sanctuary in
winter - like a rose duvet inviting
me to bury my face, switch off from
night owls, white lace

FUGITIVES

Storm clouds, hounding us
over land and sea
remorselessly...
No pause for peace;
No sanctuary;
No end in sight;
A lifetime, running away
from shadows
smouldering...
in the ruins of a lovely day,
in a heart cast aside
in haste, despair...
for taking too seriously
storm clouds, hounding us
over land and sea
remorselessly...
No pause for peace;
No sanctuary;
No end in sight;
Death, a pinprick of light
in a sickly gloom,
teasing us...
we spirits of land, sea, air,
in despair at graffiti
daubed on Heaven's door
by wannabe martyrs falling
on its holy s-word

THE STING

Hit a bee with a magazine;
it responded by chasing me
across the village green;
I ran into a church, slammed
the door shut - but the bee
found a crack, poised to attack
as I cowered in a pew,
wondering what on earth to do?
For wasn't this God's house,
the bee one of His creatures,
and wasn't I the aggressor, no
real provocation, only suspicion
it might mean me harm
so what did I think I was doing
when I raised my arm
instinctively, without thinking?
A natural reaction, I hear
you agree. So, too, that sting
taunting, haunting me still
with the merry buzzing of a bee
I never meant to kill

LEARNING CURVE

Bottom of the class for playing the fool,
always being teased for getting things wrong,
waking up every morning dreading school,
couldn't explain, no one understanding

Learning that playing the fool can be cool,
one way, at least, to make friends among peers,
still unaware that my hearing a tool
needing repair, source of worsening fears

For years I sought the truth of things in vain
and it made all the difference just to know
it was my hearing at fault, not my brain;
at last my true worth I could start to show

Life rarely comes easy, deaf or hearing...
Making the best, lessons worth the learning

FOREVER TO REMAIN

Among the world's passions piling high,
Love and Hate near breaking even,
twin towers reaching for the sky

Fear and Hope - in a cruel storm's eye;
ascent into pain, ladder to heaven
among the world's passions piling high

Though dogs of war may not pass us by,
pray Peace and Mercy be shown,
twin towers reaching for the sky

Political ambition, religion's blind eye,
spiralling us into confusion...
among the world's passions piling high

Let us plant flowers where loved-ones lie,
seeds of Joy for Remembrance sown,
twin towers reaching for the sky

Though terror its ugly tentacles try
again, again, to drag us down...
among the world's passions piling high,
twin towers reaching for the sky

SERVICE CHARGE INCLUDED

We know the time must come when we will die
but when it does, what last steps do we take?
Do we weep, pray, or simply say goodbye
to those we've come to love for love's own sake?

Dying, will at last some kind God restore
peace of mind, the innocence of a child,
or must we writhe in pain at Heaven's door,
pay the full price for being of this world?

What is repentance and what does it prove
but sheer desperation to be rescued
from an eternity without light, love...
freefall in a hell by our own lies spewed?

If truth, it play fair, come death's either shore,
why pay the ferryman a penny more?

NO NAME ON THE DOOR

A door that wasn't there before,
opening at a touch on a beautiful garden;
colour everywhere, in spring flowers,
trees whose leaves of green, red, silver, gold,
sparkle in the sunshine; every bird,
songs to sing on splendid wing flitting here and there,
so pleasing to eyes and ears seeking peace;
In tears, finding only drabness, a noisy sadness
driving us to the edge of madness, longing
for cheer, reassurance that all's not lost since Adam
(being but human) succumbed to temptation
nor great poets deceived by imagination who have
opened our hearts to paradise regained,
whether in this life or a next, daring us to pass
through a plain door, always there,
peace for the taking if only we dare choose not
(for once) to play the martyr to
a temporal morality but rise instead
to the occasion of our mortality, putting aside
humanity's natural predilection for fear,
dead set on opening a door that (how can we
be so sure?) wasn't there before...

TAKING STOCK

On Brighton pier,
a determined sea
defying my fear

Child of yesteryear
weeping for me
on Brighton pier

Letting images dear
gloss waves unruly,
defying my fear

Wind high, sky clear,
swathes of memory
on Brighton pier

Listen, and I can hear
a world in harmony
defying my fear...

Great Bear, Little Bear,
steering us through eternity;
On Brighton pier,
defying my fear

[Brighton, UK. Dec. 21st 2004]

APPENDIX I

CROCODILES IN THE WATER

A common slaughter,
Third World dying
for want of clean water

Children's laughter
turns to crying,
a common slaughter

Each young-old grafter
grown sick of trying
for want of clean water

At some capital altar,
disciples denying
a common slaughter

A 21st century arena
found sadly lacking...
for want of clean water

Through gold teeth, eager
summit tipplers belying
a common slaughter
for want of clean water

Note: In some copies of *The Third Eye* there is an error in line 1, last stanza.

APPENDIX II

NATIONAL TRUST OUTING
(For Andrew B.)

On my way downstairs, I paused
to look at a portrait on the wall
and it winked at me, opened
its mouth and said (laughingly),
"Yes, I too was gay in my day
although the word not invented
nor times quite ready to receive
the unseemly likes of a common
painter and his patron lover - so
we had to lie, indulge in subterfuge;
no one had the faintest idea,
certainly not the family (wife and
children included) or that ogre
Establishment whose inner circle
I was free enough to tread, so long
as I dared not bring it into disrepute
by word or deed. Oh, I loved them
well enough, indeed. But it's not for
love of those I pose – radiating,
I suspect, an inner happiness?
Ah, yes, you understand. It is my
lover's brush, exploring mind
and soul, touching what makes life
real, no trappings and trimmings
comprising Society's queer notion
of propriety, political expediency
or even an image of home fires
burning - but Love, in all its
rampant glory, telling my story
here and now, for whoever might
care to consider, critically, a glow
in the cheek, lift of the eyebrow,

crook of the knee, hands pointedly
showing off slender fingers, touches
invariably missed in critique, put down
to art's mystique, few appreciating
the intimacy between lover and lover,
bouncing off each other long after
the oils runs dry, spoils of eternity."

In my own time I descended,
feeling befriended

Note: This is a slightly revised/amended version than appears in
some copies of *The Third Eye*.

APPENDIX III

HITTING HOME

Flung open the door, smile on the face,
fist at the jaw, fallen to the floor,
waiting for more;
Eyes closed, mind shut tight to it all,
homing in on a single happy time
before things fell apart;
Breaking heart in pieces on the mat,
angry tongue making the lips bleed;
a bad day at the office;
Blows lessen, cease; a thousand terrors
and sick with humiliation
for this love of ours;
You'll go upstairs, slam the bedroom
door, be down in about half an hour
for supper - in what temper?
Tomorrow, a rose; any tears, yours (on
these so-bruised cheeks) - forgiveness
again, compassion or passion?
If I try to pray, even God asks why I stay
and when I confess no idea, a dear
familiar voice calls me a liar...
Where I found strength to love you,
I must find the same to leave you
or be like your rose

In a smashed vase

Note: In some copies of *The Third Eye*, this poem appears with a misprint, line 14.

214

ACKNOWLEDGEMENTS:

I would like to thank all those editors and publishers who have included my work in various poetry magazines and anthologies since I first began submitting for publication in 1993. I would also like to thank friends and colleagues for their support. A special thank you to Internet friends and contacts, many of whom I have never met in person; their Instant Message comments and e-mails have provided encouragement and inspiration since I first went online in 1998 and, hopefully, will continue to do so.

Roger Noel Taber